XFV-12

Thrust-Augmented Wing V/STOL Fighter Concept

Hugh Harkins

Copyright © 2020 Hugh Harkins

All rights reserved.

ISBN: 1-903630-91-6
ISBN-13: 978-1-903630-91-4

XFV-12

Thrust-Augmented Wing V/STOL Fighter Concept

© Hugh Harkins 2020

Centurion Publishing

United Kingdom

ISBN 10: 1-903630-91-6
ISBN 13: 978-1-903630-91-4

This volume first published in 2020

The Author is identified as the copyright holder of this work under sections 77 and 78 of the Copyright Designs and Patents Act 1988

Cover design © Centurion Publishing & KDP

Page layout, concept and design © Centurion Publishing

All rights reserved. No part of this publication may be reproduced, stored in a retrieval system, transmitted in any form, or by any means, electronic, mechanical or photocopied, recorded or otherwise, without the written permission of the publisher

This research paper has adopted the Harvard Manual of Style for referencing. It has, however, not always been possible to adopt a standard referencing format for some of the primary source documentation

For Sean
Our Man on the Moon
1990-2020

CONTENTS

	INTRODUCTION	vii
1	XFV-12A THRUST AUGMENTED WING	1
2	DEVELOPMENT, STRUCTURAL, FUNCTIONAL, STATIC & DYNAMIC TETHERED HOVER AND DIAGNOSTIC TESTING	51
3	DIAGNOSTIC & REDEVELOPMENT PHASES – XFV-12B/C	73
4	GLOSSARY	85
5	BIBLIOGRAPHY	87

INTRODUCTION

Conceived in the early 1970's, the Rockwell International XFV-12A was an evolution of research efforts aimed at bringing to fruition a supersonic fighter aircraft capable of conducting V/STOL (Vertical/Short Take-Off and Landing) operations from the deck of a surface vessel or terrestrial base. A major goal for the XFV-12A research aircraft program, employing thrust augmented wing technology to achieve vertical lift, was to produce a practical design endowed with a relatively benign V/STOL footprint.

The volume details the genesis of the XFV-12A program through static and dynamic hover testing of the prototype air vehicle at the NASA (National Aeronautics and Space Administration) Langley Research Centre Impact Dynamic Research Facility to the redevelopment program that spawned the XFV-12B and XFV-12C designs. These latter designs did not proceed beyond the drawing board prior to the XFV-12 programs ultimate cancellation in 1981. Post XFV-12 cancellation, Rockwell International was contracted by NASA Ames Research Center to conduct design studies into aerodynamic technology for a single-cruise engine V/STOL fighter/attack aircraft, building on work conducted during the XFV-12 program – this work was conducted in the period June 1981 to February 1982.

The volume is supported by photographs, renderings, technical drawings and specification charts from the aircraft designer and research institutions. At times there has been a deliberate switch from metric measurements to the fore and imperial measurements secondary to imperial to the fore and metric secondary. This has been done to ensure 100% accuracy in primary measurement reporting from respective designer/research organisations, whereas secondary measurements may, at times, be rounded up or down.

1

XFV-12A THRUST AUGMENTED WING

The Rockwell International XFV-12A was conceived as a USN (United States Navy) funded V/STOL (Vertical Short Take-Off and Landing) naval fighter aircraft concept in the early 1970's. The technology demonstrator program was intended to investigate the suitability of the thrust-augmented wing/canard ejector technology concept for employment in a future V/STOL naval fighter aircraft optimised for the air-superiority role. The program was intended to field an aircraft designed for research purposes, not to constitute the prototype of a design intended for serial production (NASC).

Thrust augmentation in aircraft design was not in itself a new technology concept. The other major thrust augmentation research program in the 1970's was the NASA (National Aeronautics and Space Administration) Augmenter Wing Jet STOL (Short Take-Off and Landing) research program. This utilised a De Havilland C-8A Buffalo transport aircraft that was modified to produce around half its available thrust through wing trailing-edge mounted augmenters, with the balance produced by nacelle mounted rotating nozzles (Aiken, 1977).

An early utilisation for thrust augmenter technology was to direct a layer of cool air over the engine nozzle of jet powered aircraft. This practice revealed the presence of moderate increases in thrust, considered beneficial for direct lift through the process of thrust augmentation. This was employed by the Lockheed XV-4A VTOL (Vertical Take-Off and Landing) research aircraft developed in the late 1960's. Thrust augmentation research work had ramped up from the late 1960's, with emphasis placed on development of a thrust augmenting ejector optimised for production of higher augmentation ratios than hitherto considered. The AFRL (Air Force Research Laboratory) was instrumental in advancing such research work. The basic research conducted at the AFRL fed into the concept formulations for a USN V/STOL research aircraft program that would utilise thrust augmentation for lift in the VTOL flight regimes (Lopez *et al*, 1979). This would lead directly to a technology development program for the USN in cooperation with Rockwell International Corporations Columbus Aircraft Division, Ohio. The research aircraft/technology demonstrator was to be designed as a supersonic fighter aircraft, which would employ thrust augmenting ejectors on the wing surfaces in order to produce lift for vertical take-off and landings and for operations in the hover flight regime. This concept would become known as the TAW (Thrust Augmenting Wing).

Rockwell XFV-12A Thrust Augmented Wing prototype. Rockwell (Boeing)

Top: The first Kestrel FGA.1 subsonic V/STOL strike fighter during trials with the Tripartite Evaluation Squadron formed by the United Kingdom, United States (the US designated the aircraft XV-6A) and West Germany. **Above:** The Kestrel evolved into the Harrier GR.1, which was further evolved into the Sea Harrier (Indian Navy FRS.51 illustrated) as a carrier based strike fighter, initially for the British Royal Navy. The USMC adopted the AV-8A/C Americanised variant of the Harrier GR.1 as an attack aircraft with a secondary day short-range fighter capability for operations from USN amphibious assault ships. BAE Systems

While there were many paper design studies for supersonic V/STOL aircraft on both sides of the Atlantic during the 1960's, it was in Europe that such concepts were brought to fruition, in regard to research aircraft. The supersonic Mirage III V (flight tested during 1965-1966) V/STOL design (top) was developed from the Dassault Balzac V/STOL research aircraft. The concept was ultimately abandoned as technically unsuitable, requiring eight RB162 lift engines to achieve vertical flight and a single engine for cruise flight. The Soviets were experimenting with supersonic fighter aircraft designs capable of extremely short take-off. The Sukhoi T-58VD research aircraft (bottom) was equipped with lift thrust engines, complementing the cruise turbojet engines to lift the aircraft into the air after a short run. This concept, tested during 1966-1967, did not progress beyond evaluation. Dassault/Sukhoi

The idea of a supersonic multirole strike fighter capable of V/STOL operation had been formulated in Europe in the 1960's, with such programs as the British Hawker Siddeley P.1154 and the French Dassault Balzac. The former, envisioned as a supersonic V/STOL design for service from British aircraft carrier decks, was cancelled at the design stage and replaced by the McDonnell Douglas Phantom FG.1 (F-4K) which went on to serve the RN (Royal Navy) until transferred to the RAF in the late 1970's, joining that services fleet of Phantom FGR.2 (F-4M). The Balzac, which progressed to the flight test stage, was further developed, leading to the Mirage III V (these designs evolved in-line with the NATO NBMR.3 requirement for a supersonic V/STOL capable strike fighter, ultimately cancelled). Like the Balzac, the Mirage III V (achieved a speed of Mach 2.2 in 1966) proved to be overly complex and was cancelled – the design required no less than eight RB162 lift engines to achieve vertical flight and a single engine for cruise flight. The subsonic Hawker Siddeley P.1127, which evolved into the Kestrel and Harrier subsonic V/STOL strike fighter aircraft, had demonstrated the ability to operate from a ships deck in the early 1960's. Shipboard operations would later become the norm for the AV-8A/C variant of the Harrier operated by the USMC (United States Marine Corp) and the British Aerospace (later BAE Systems) Sea Harrier FRS.1, developed in the late 1970's for service with the RN. However, the desire for a supersonic V/STOL capability remained extant through the 1970's, with a number of concepts of various technology sets – direct lift, lift + cruise etc., and, of course, the TAW – evolving, albeit, as paper designs.

As attention focused on potential benefits of V/STOL capable aircraft operations from sea surface platforms, the US Naval Material Command, on 15 November 1971, forwarded a request for proposals in letter form to a number of aviation design companies. This called for submission of separate V/STOL design proposals that would be capable of conducting a subsonic multipurpose role or a supersonic capable fighter aircraft design with in inherent attack capability – in effect a V/STOL multirole strike fighter capable of air to surface, interception and air superiority missions. As well as operating from aircraft carriers the V/STOL designs were to be capable of operating from significantly smaller vessels of around 12500 tons, then forwarded as the Sea Control Ship concept (Rockwell International XFV-12A D&DP, 1981).

The augmented thrust lift and control system was developed at Rockwell's Aircraft Division, Columbus, Ohio. Although primarily intended for the XFV-12A research aircraft, these studies took into consideration such a concepts viability for installation in an operational V/STOL multirole fighter design capable of operating from large aircraft carriers down to small carrier vessels of around 12500 tons – Sea Control Ship. Such vessels would be capable of rendering support to naval task force operations – ASW (Anti-Submarine Warfare) and air defence – naval assault forces – ground forces air support and air defence. The invitation to forward bids for the USN V/STOL supersonic fighter research prototype program was the platform required for Rockwell to push the TAW concept to the fore (Delany & Jenkins, 1976).

In the period covering the first half of the 1970's there was a plethora of V/STOL fighter concepts being pushed by various design houses. This design, employing a battery of lift jets to enable vertical flight, is shown operating from a small surface platform, indicating a similar role to that envisioned for the XFV-12A. NASA

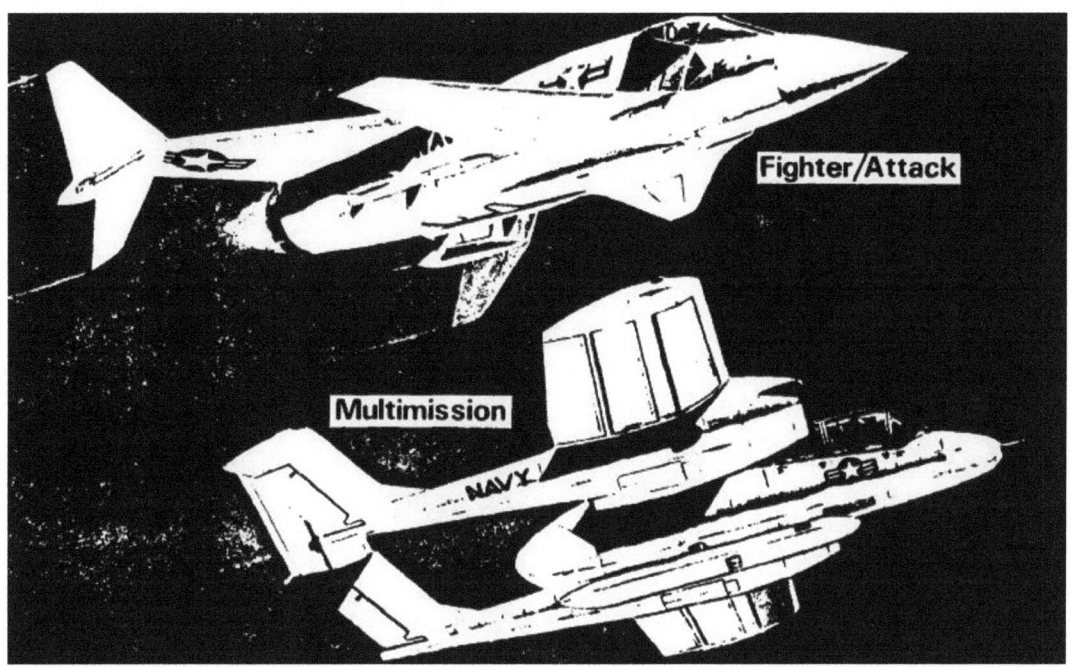

Poor quality copy of artist rendering of Rockwell International's thrust augmented wing proposals to meet the V/STOL fighter/attack and V/STOL multi-mission aircraft for service from the Sea Control Ship concept mooted in the early 1970's. Rockwell International (Boeing)

Rockwell International submitted proposals to address fighter/attack and multi-mission concepts, all featuring derivatives of Rockwell's TAW concept to produce lift. Rockwell's TAW concept, which centred on a multi-dimensional thrust augmenting ejector system (Lopez *et al*, 1979), promised a solution to some of the problems associated with V/STOL operations form a ships deck, not least of which was the hard footprint of thrust induced detriments against the deck in VTOL operations. Rockwell's TAW concept was, in October 1972, selected to proceed, in regard to the supersonic V/STOL fighter design. The focus was in advancing technology applicable to a V/STOL aircraft rather than to produce a design intended for serial production following successful testing (Rockwell International XFV-12A D&DP, 1981). Rockwell was awarded a contract, N00019-73-C-0053 – for development and build of two XFV-12A's – under the Fighter Attack Technology Prototype Program (Stewart, 1987). Each of these aircraft was to be designed so they could be configured for either CTOL (Conventional Take-Off and Landing) or V/STOL operations. In CTOL flight demonstrations the aircraft was to be powered by a single Pratt & Whitney YF401-PW-400 turbofan engine, utilising afterburner with balanced beam nozzle exhaust. When configured for V/STOL demonstration/testing the XFV-12A would be powered by a single YF401-PW-400 fitted out with V/STOL specific equipment, close-coupled to the diverter complex, itself coupled to the augmenters. When configured for V/STOL operation the engine was capable of being utilised for conventional flight operations with the engine operated up to intermediate power settings (non-afterburning). The two engine option was selected to reduce development costs and reduce demonstration time as it negated the need for the engine adapted for V/STOL operations to be developed and qualified for operations in afterburner mode, a trait then required for supersonic flight in conventional flight operations (Delany & Jenkins, 1976).

Artwork showing an XFV-12A derivative vehicle operating in the VTOL mode from a surface vessel platform. Rockwell International (Boeing)

The YF401 was selected as it was a modern turbofan engine with acceptable intermediate (non-afterburning) thrust ratings, with mixed flow (engine core and fan), dimensions that were compatible with the planned aircraft design and its availability within the planned program development timeframe. For the engine to be used in V/STOL demonstrations the conventional exhaust nozzle would be replaced by a translating plug nozzle shroud complex with a diverter exit system developed by the engine parent company, Pratt & Whitney, through a joint contract from the USN and Rockwell International Corporation (Swavely, 1974 & Delany & Jenkins, 1976). The engine exhaust gases would be expelled aft through the plug nozzle to facilitate operation in conventional flight (Delany & Jenkins, 1976). Under Newton's laws of Action and Reaction the air flow directed through the shroud complex would result in a phenomenon in the ejector equating to a force that was equal, but opposite, to the change of momentum in the drawn in air (Rockwell International XFV-12A D&DP, 1981). When operating in VTOL mode the exhaust gas would be diverted to the wing and canard mounted thrust augmenter (lift) systems via a complex of ducting – the overall exhaust gas collection and circulation complex (Delany & Jenkins, 1976). A major objective set for the program, other than demonstrating the viability of the thrust augmentation, was to produce a system with the minimum possible leaks and pressure loss (Delany & Jenkins, 1976).

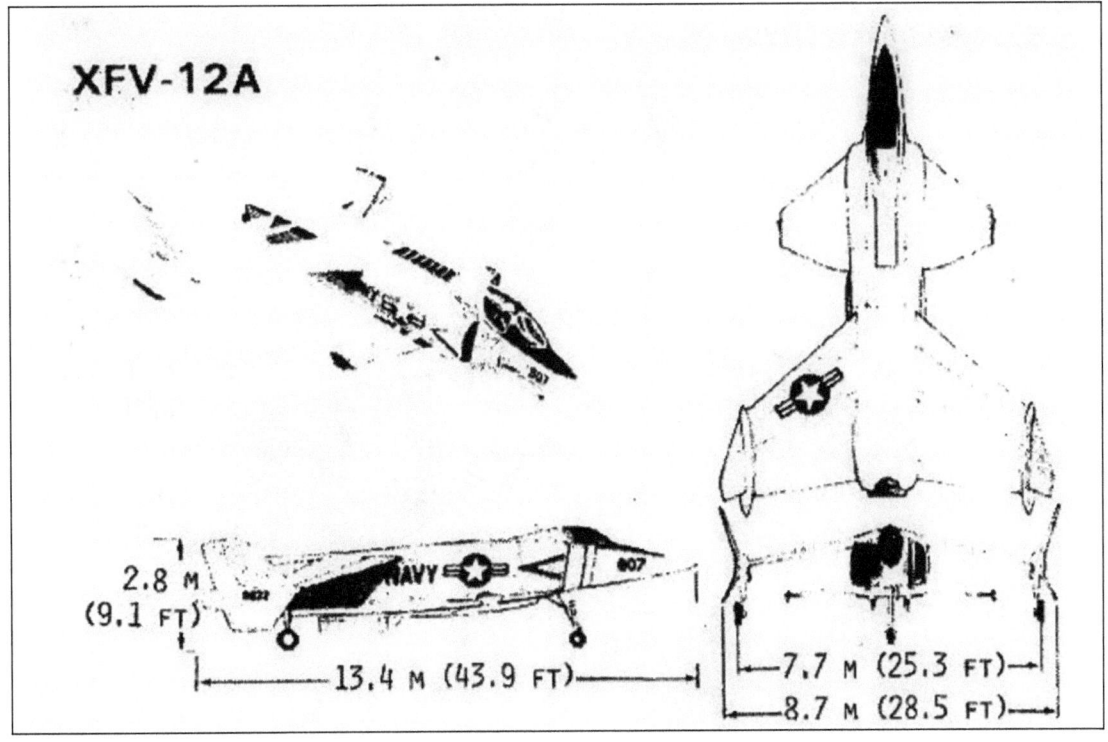

General arrangement of the XFV-12A showing basic dimensions. Culpepper *et al*, 1979

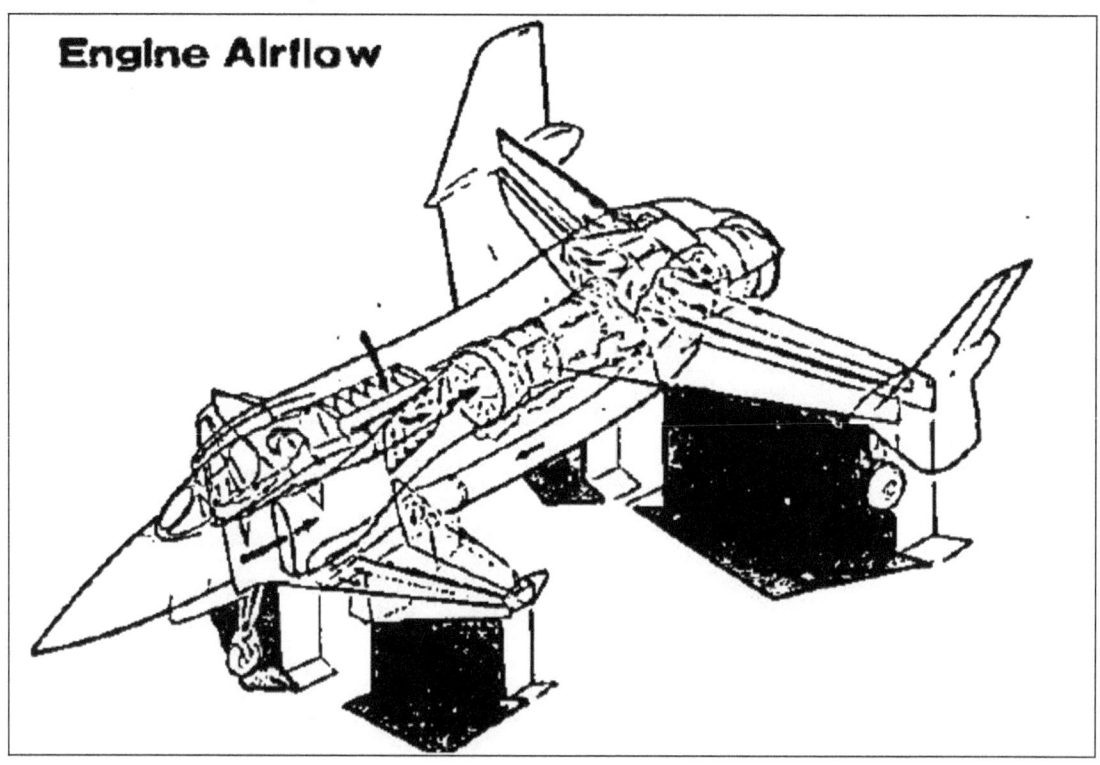

XFV-12A ghosted view (top) and XFV-12A propulsion system in VTOL mode (above). Rockwell International (Boeing)

The XFV-12A underwent an extensive development program from conceptual design through tethered hover testing to diagnostic redevelopment. The aircraft was designed by Rockwell Corporation and developed and built at the corporations Columbus Aircraft Division, Ohio. It was intended to mature the concept to the flight demonstration stage to evaluate the thrust-augmented wing concept in various flight modes, vertical take-off, conversion to horizontal flight and conventional flight (Murphy *et al* c1970's).

The basic design concept adopted for the XFV-12A was that of a high set main wing and low set forward canard fore-planes, with vertical surfaces on the main wingtips in lieu of vertical tails surfaces, which were absent (Murphy *et al* c1970's, Culpepper *et al*, 1979, Rockwell International XFV-12A D&DP, 1981 & Leon, 1982). Smaller surfaces were incorporated into the design of the canards (Leon, 1982).

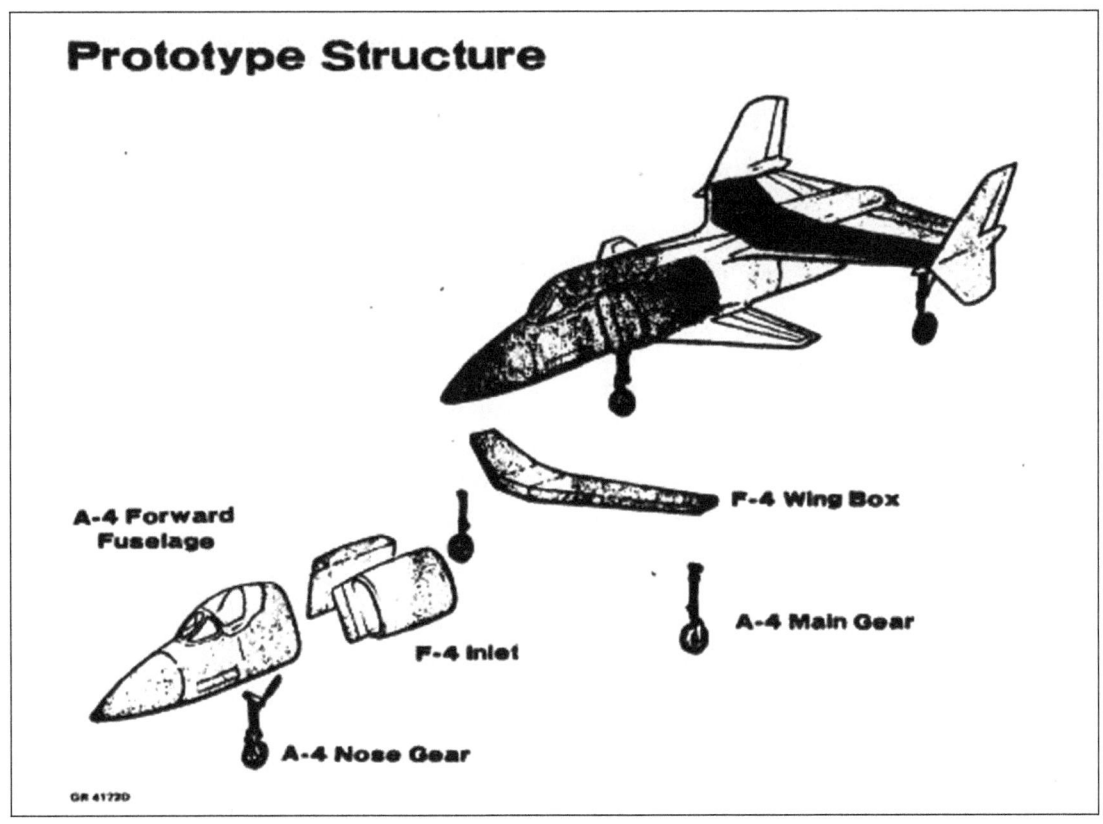

This page: Basic structural components of the XFV-12A, as sourced from A-4 Skyhawk and F-4 Phantom II legacy aircraft designs. Rockwell International (Boeing)

Two views of a NASA XFV-12A model showing the basic layout of the aircraft – main wing, forward canard and vertical surfaces on the main wing tips in lieu of conventional vertical tail surface(s). NASA

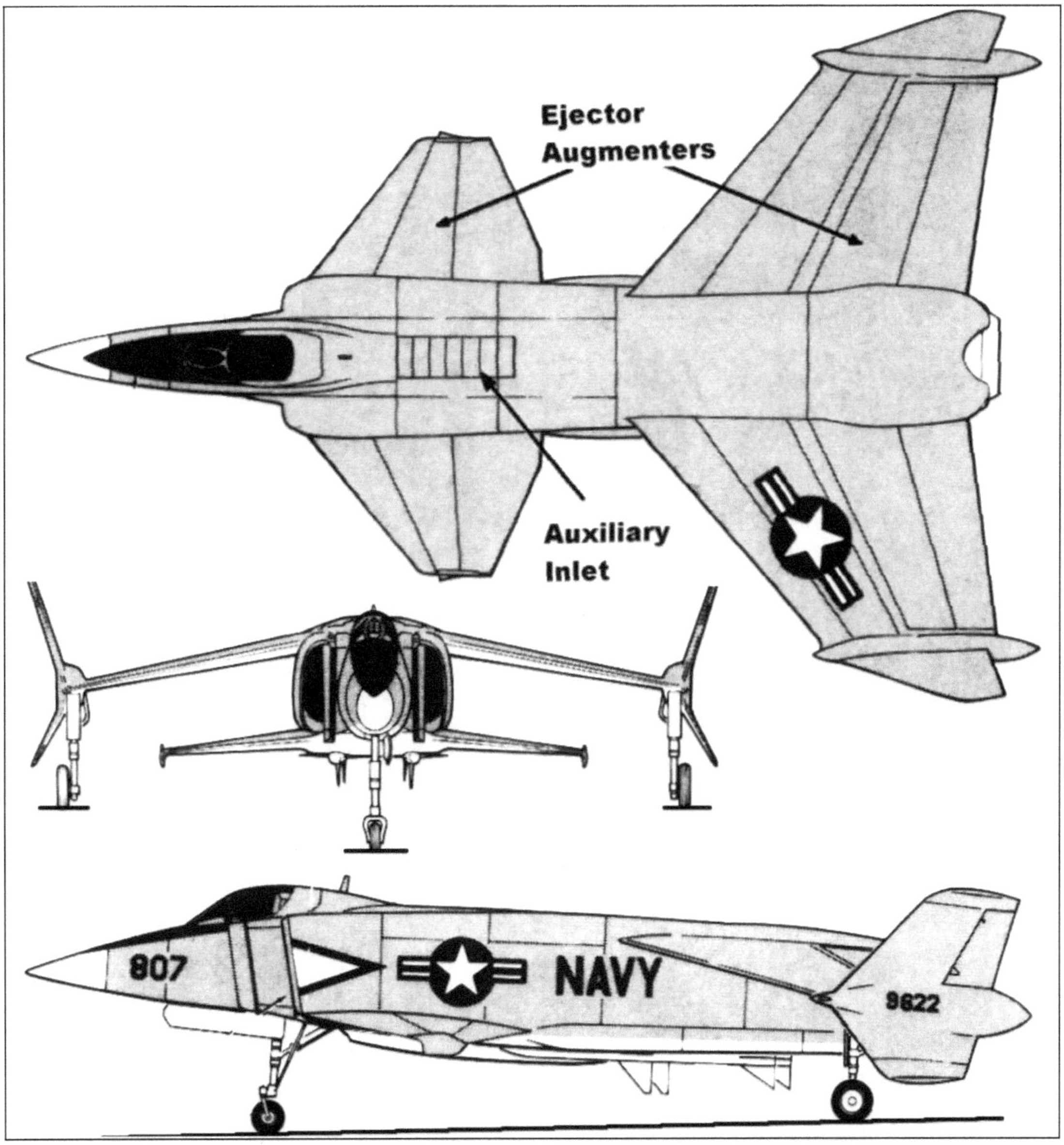

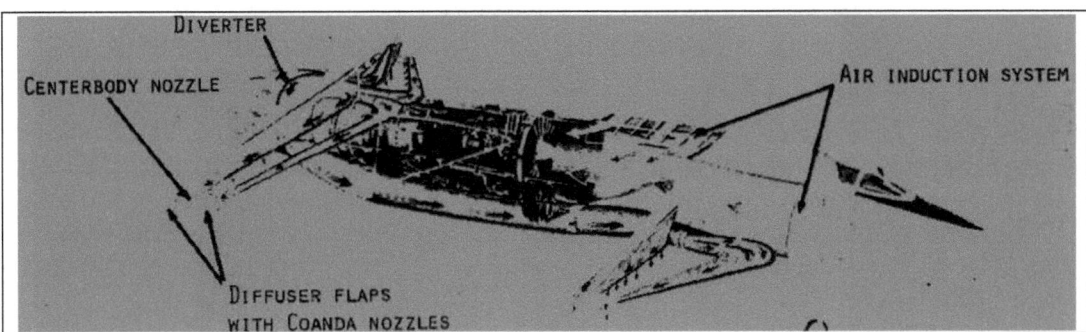

XFV-12A 3-view general arrangement (top) and airflow induction, distribution and exit system diagram (above). Rolls Royce/Rockwell International (Boeing)

The design incorporated much new technology, including the use of carbon-epoxy on the wing skins (Watts *et al*, 1985), but, to reduce program costs and speed up development, the XFV-12A incorporated existing components from several legacy aircraft designs. This included a McDonnell Douglas A-4C Skyhawk light attack aircraft forward fuselage section (TO FS 180 70), A-4 cockpit section, A-4 nose section, A-4C nose and main undercarriage units, a modified McDonnell Douglas F-4A Phantom II multirole strike fighter air inlet system – the variable and fixed ramps, the actuators and a system for boundary layer bleed – integrated with the subsonic bifurcated diffuser designed for the XFV-12A. The F-4A inlet cowls were modified – available width was reduced in-line with meeting the airflow requirements for the YF401-PW-400 turbofan engine, which differed from the twin General Electric J79 turbojet engine arrangement in the F-4A. The F-4 style vertical ramp intakes were chosen not just because of availability, but also due to the requirement to reduce to a minimal the potential for re-ingestion of hot gas from the canard mounted augmenter complex (Delany & Jenkins, 1976 & Rockwell International XFV-12A D&DP, 1981).

The lateral primary intakes and upper fuselage auxiliary intake that formed the XFV-12A air induction system are shown to advantage in the NASA free flight model, which underwent testing during 1974. Nasa 74-5303

The air induction complex feeding the engines was trifurcated, consisting of the two primary F-4A (modified) vertical ramp air inlets (described above), positioned laterally on the external fuselage. This led to a bifurcated subsonic diffuser, along with a single auxiliary compressor inlet positioned on the fuselage upper surface, just aft of the cockpit section. The primary function of the latter intake was to provide additional air feed to the engines during VTOL operations (Murphy *et al* c1970's, Delany & Jenkins, 1976 & Rockwell International XFV-12A D&DP, 1981). The air induction system inlets, with fixed cowls and ramps, are actuated to allow for variation of the inlet throat area for more efficient feeding of air – different flight modes requiring differing variations of air feed. Their positioning on the fuselage upper surface was selected as it was considered the optimum position in order to reduce to a minimum the possibility of airflow re-ingestion when operating in vertical take-off mode and reduced to a minimum the potential for foreign object ingestion during ground operations and vertical take-off and landings. Post-test results indicated that only a small amount of re-ingestion encountered had occurred through the upper fuselage inlet. Positioning the inlet on the fuselage upper surface rather than the fuselage under surface would also have aided studies in weapon/ordnance layouts, which would have been fuselage mounted had the program proceeded to such demonstrations (Leon, 1982).

Overall the air induction system was designed for marginal engine distortion whilst providing acceptable performance when operating at transonic speed up to the maximum Mach number (Delany & Jenkins, 1976). The induction system was evaluated by use of a 0.2 scale-model (low-speed). Initial thermodynamics testing was conducted at the Thermodynamics Laboratory under static conditions (Delany & Jenkins, 1976). Data obtained from small-scale model tests was verified through a series of full-scale tests conducted at the Columbus Aircraft Division's engine test facility. This test phase involved mating a YF401-PW-400 engine with an XFV-12A forward fuselage section (this was basically complete with the exception of the canards, which were omitted) (Delany & Jenkins, 1976). In order to operate the engine over the full spectrum of operating conditions expected for an operational design, a standard YF401-PW-400 was used as this was capable of operating in afterburner, whilst the YF401, when fitted with the V/STOL specific modifications was not capable of operating in afterburner (noted above). The engine tests indicated good performance over the full spectrum – from idle up to afterburner (Delany & Jenkins, 1976).

Top: 0.2 scale air induction model during low speed tests at the Columbus Aircraft Division Thermodynamics Laboratory on 30 August 1973. Bottom: Full scale inlet testing conducted at Rockwell International's Columbus Aircraft Division's engine test facility. Rockwell International (Boeing)

Close up of the port canard on the XFV-12A prototype. NASA L-78-4176

XFV-12A cockpit canopy in the open position during the dynamic hover test phase in June 1978. NASA L-78-4175

One area where full-scale testing indicated notable differences in data obtained through small scale model tests was that pressure recovery in the full-scale tests were moderately in excess of those obtained in the 0.2-scale model tests. The 0.2-scale model tests confirmed the pre-test estimate of a 96% pressure recovery value. Full-scale inlet/engine tests confirmed the trait of high pressure recovery at the inlet when in VTOL mode, as well as distortion levels not too dissimilar to that demonstrated in the 0.2-scale model tests (Delany & Jenkins, 1976).

Other F-4 components incorporated in the XFV-12A design included the activation system, main wing box (now constructed as a 'Gr/E with nomex honeycomb core wing to fuselage box' (Baumann & Swedlov, 1981) along with A-4 components incorporated into the plumbing system and appropriation of various other A-4 equipment. Much of the cockpit systems, instrumentation and pilot escape system – zero-zero ejection seat – as well as elements of hydraulic, fuel, environmental, electrical and electronic systems, were sourced from existing USN service aircraft (Rockwell International XFV-12A D&DP, 1981 & Delany & Jenkins, 1976).

When the canard configuration was adopted for the XFV-12A it was decided to position the canards below the plane of the main wing. This went against the majority of research data that suggested the optimum location/configuration for canards was positioned higher and close-coupled in relation to the wings. Rockwell studies had concluded that, while this was promising for cruise flight and conventional take-off – requiring 15-20° flap deflection – positioning the canards lower was better for the STOL flight regime, which required flap deflection greater than 30° (Stewart, 1987).

The incorporation of canard foreplanes, apart from their contribution to the lift system, allowed the overall area of the main wing to be reduced without a corresponding reduction in aircraft manoeuvrability – this was a result of the wings and canard surfaces simultaneously providing lift. The canard layout also enhanced the viability of the characteristic wingtip mounted vertical surfaces, which were incorporated into the XFV-12A design to enhance directional stability at various angles of attack, reduce airframe drag through lift, enhanced longitudinal stability and potentially reduce the aerodynamic center-shift as the aircraft moved from subsonic to supersonic speed regimes (Leon, 1982). The vertical surfaces had three major functions – enhancement of aircraft longitudinal stability, enhancing effectiveness of wing aspect ratio and provision of directional stability and control characteristics (Rockwell International XFV-12A D&DP, 1981). The first two of these functions aids in reducing required wingspan (noted above), and, by default, aircraft weight. A number of research efforts were undertaken for the wingtip mounted vertical surfaces, including high angle of attack on a small-scale model. Results were limited and required testing on large-scale models if conclusive data was to be obtained (Leon, 1982).

A 0.3 scale canard model and a 0.2 scale wing model were tested in Rockwell's Columbus Aircraft Division thermodynamics division to determine characteristics that would be applicable to the full-scale canard and wing (Delany & Jenkins, 1976). The basic canard design was formulated on a NACA 66-008375 (MOD) with an incidence of 0° and 5° dihedral. The wing design had its origins in the FUS STA 27354, WP-22081 & FUS STA 4000, WP-18.75, with incidence P30 and dihedral, minus 10° (Rockwell International XFV-12A D&DP, 1981).

XFV-12A project 470, during testing in building 645 in 1974. This NASA test model provides a good representation of the high main wing low canard layout of the XFV-12A. NASA

CANARD DATA

```
ORIGIN - C ∂WP · 35.00, BP 3750 & LE ∂ FS 133.00
INCIDENCE           = 0°
DIHEDRAL            = -5°
S_EXP               = 82.7 FT²_ACT · 82.385 FT²_PROJ
AR                  = 1.7654_ACT  1.7567_PROJ
B/2_ACT             = 72.50 IN
C_R                 = 128.00 IN
C_T                 = 36.26 IN
Λ_LE TRUE           = 39°46
AIRFOIL             NACA 66-008375 (MOD)
```
(FUS STA 100)

WING SHOWN IN FUSELAGE REF SYSTEM

WING DATA

```
ORIGIN · FUS. STA 273.54 WP + 22.061 & FUS. STA 400.0, WP + 18.75

INCIDENCE       1°30
DIHEDRAL        -10°
S_PROJ          293.789 FT²
S_ACT           298.323 FT²
AR_PROJ         2.085
C_R             196.370 IN
C_T             88.516 IN                    FRP
```

Top: Technical characteristics of the XFV-12A canard. Bottom: Technical characteristics of the XFV-12A wing. Rockwell International XFV-12A D&DP, 1981

Assembly work on the vertical tail surfaces (incorporating the main undercarriage units) on the XFV-12A working mock-up at Rockwell's Columbus Aircraft Division in January 1973. Rockwell International (Boeing)

XFV-12

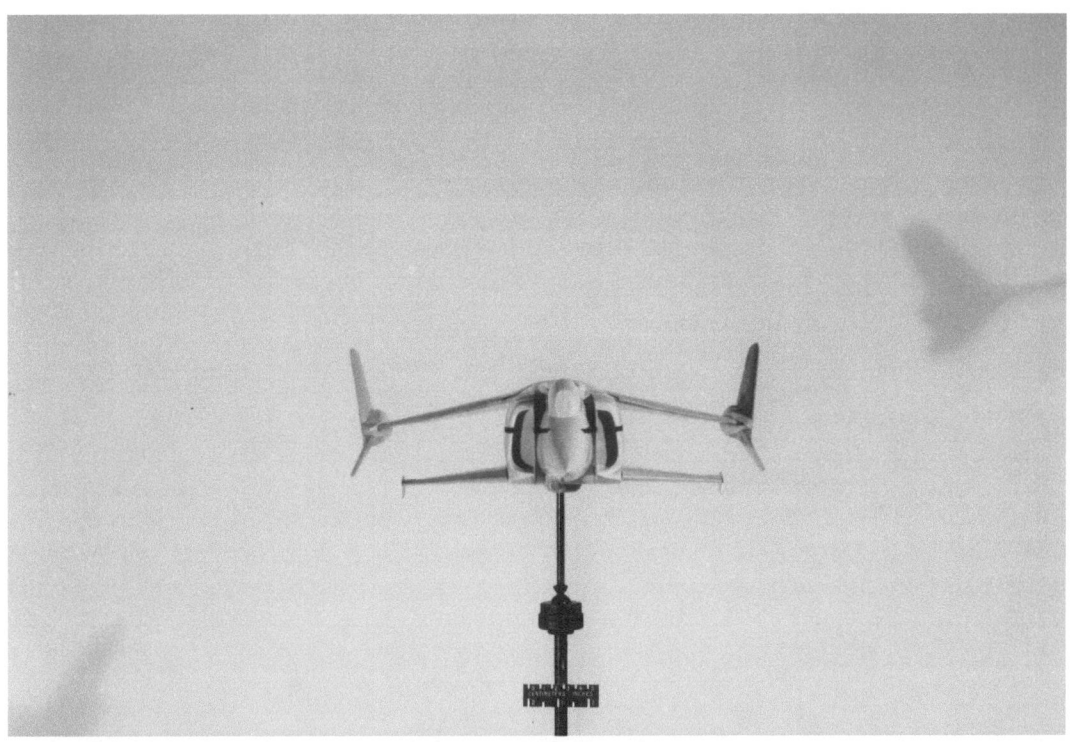

Previous page top: Head-on view of a NASA XFV-12A test model – dating from 1974 – demonstrating to advantage the high main wing/low canard and wingtip vertical surface layout inherent in the XFV-12A design. Previous page bottom: Installation on XFV-12A airframe of a standard YF401-PW-400 engine – lacking the modifications for V/STOL operation – 22 January 1973. This page: The canard mounted augmenter system on the XFV-12A prototype, 29 April 1977. NASA/Rockwell International (Boeing)

Universally the rule of thumb for V/STOL aircraft design is that the VTOL element of the mission required significantly higher thrust than was required for the conventional flight phases of the mission. The TAW concept promised a sea change in that the unfavourable design traits of V/STOL aircraft would be partly reduced. Among the benefits was the ability to operate with a reduced thrust output power plant in comparison to what would be required for V/STOL aircraft of comparable mission capability that employed thrust deflection. This promised superior thrust to weight efficiency for the TAW concept during conventional cruise flight (Rockwell International XFV-12A D&DP, 1981).

XFV-12

H-356-94-3J   12-1-72

H-356-94-3N   12-1-72

Page 25-26: YF401-PW-400 engine development tests included ground based testing and system integration testing on the XFV-12A. Rockwell International (Boeing)

As had been the case with airframe development, it was decided to adopt existing engine technology. In this context it was decided to power the XFV-12A with a single Pratt & Whitney YF401-PW-400 turbofan engine (Murphy *et al* c1970's, Culpepper *et al*, 1979 & Delany & Jenkins, 1976). This would be without modification, other than to those areas applicable to VTOL operations. This involved the standard exhaust nozzle arrangement being replaced with a translating plug nozzle arrangement, which incorporated a shroud and led to the diverter system. The basic operation modes of the complex consisted of: 1. the engine thrust divert mode (for VTOL) operations, in which the gas flow from the engine is diverted through ducting to the augmentation system. 2. A transition mode for conversion from VTOL to conventional flight, with the gas flow from the engine being arranged through the diverter system and the translating plug nozzle, more or less continuous and homogenous back-pressure to the engine being maintained. 3. A horizontal thrust mode for conventional cruise flight (Rockwell International XFV-12A D&DP, 1981). In conventional flight mode the exhaust gas flow from the engine is directed aft and exits through the translating shroud nozzle complex at the rear of the engine before being ejected through the translating plug nozzle (Rockwell International XFV-12A D&DP, 1981 & Delany & Jenkins, 1976).

XFV-12

The engine development was conducted through testing of analytical models, a series of operations simulations and full-scale engine testing on ground based rigs, ultimately leading to system integration testing on the XFV-12A (Delany & Jenkins, 1976). In 1976, the value for thrust to weight ratio for the YF401 engine intended for the XFV-12A was put at 0.72, with a net thrust to weight ratio in augmentation mode of 1.55. A mean exit velocity for the augmented air flow was put at 130 m/s (427 ft./s), which was less predictions for then current direct lift V/STOL systems (NASA Advances in Engineering Science Vol.4, 1976).

At an engine thrust power stetting of 16,500 lb. (~7484 kg) for the YF401 engine, this calculated to ~10,850 lb. (~4921 kg) and ~9,730 lb. (~4413 kg) of lift for the wing and canard respectively, for a combined total lift thrust of 20,580 lb. (~9335 kg). It was found that the gasses from the YF401 exhaust was diverted to the wing augmenters, 47.5%, and canard augmenters 52.5%. Calculations showed a level of thrust loss through leaks and pressure loss was 8% for the wing mounted augmenter, rising to 12% for the canard mounted augmenters (Murphy *et al* c1970's).

Lockheed XV-4A Hummingbird. NASA

ENGINE/EJECTOR INTERFACE – In regard to high performance jet powered aircraft, the first major application of thrust-augmentation to achieve lift was the Lockheed XV-4A Hummingbird research aircraft. This emerged with what was referred to as a two-door block and turn diverter. The XFV-12A design team, benefiting from advances in technology and knowledge in the field, incorporated what was referred to as a sliding-sleeve augmenter system into design concepts (Lowry, c1979 in Lopez *et al*, 1979). Calculations showed that a number of trade-offs had to be accepted with the installation of the diverter valve. This included a weight increase for the host aircraft of around 200 lb. (~91 kg) (the diverter valve system incorporated in the XFV-12A had a weight in the region of 400 lb. (~181 kg)), which was mostly aft of the aircraft centre of gravity. Calculated loss in gas pressure was around 3%, with a further loss of around 1% due to exhaust gas leaks. Another area of compromise that could result in weight increase and or thrust loss, included the potential need to increase the engine exhaust nozzle area over that of a corresponding CTOL (Conventional Take-Off and Landing) design. Going into the 1980's, a major design deficiency existed in that a practical solution had not been found to address the indelible fact that, at then current technology levels, operation of the engine in afterburner mode was not compatible with safe and efficient operation of a diverter valve (Lowry, c1979 in Lopez *et al*, 1979) – a serious detriment for an aircraft designed as a multirole or air combat fighter.

As with all VTOL and V/STOL aircraft designs, the transition phase that takes the aircraft from vertical (powered lift) to horizontal (conventional/wing-borne) flight was a major research/design challenge. Incorporation of a quad-ejector configuration in the XFV-12A enabled, in theory, avoidance of problems that effected the XV-4A research aircraft program, such as extremely adverse effects on very-low-speed pitch and yaw flight characteristics (Lowry, c1979 in Lopez *et al*, 1979).

DIVERTER SYSTEM – The power plant of aircraft utilising thrust augmentation for lift required not only provision of the thrust required for successful conventional flight, but also to serve as the source for hot gas channelled to the augmenter system to provide lift when operating in the VTOL mode (sometimes referred to as the ejector powered mode). When operating in VTOL mode, exhaust gasses from the engine are channelled through a diverter valve in the ejector complex (Lowry, c1979 in Lopez *et al*, 1979).

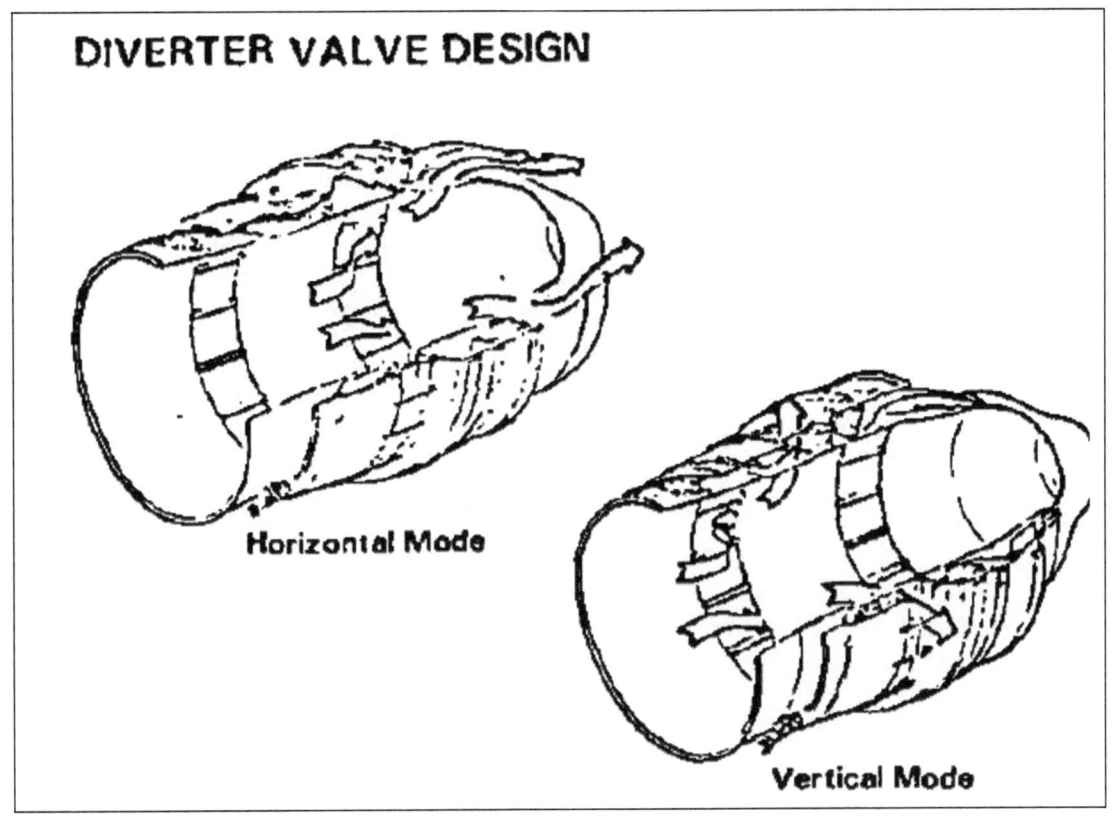

Diverter unit for XFV-12A power plant shown in horizontal and vertical modes. Rockwell International XFV-12A D&DP, 1981

The primary function of the diverter unit, which was composed of a translating nozzle, doors for the diverter complex and a complex to collect gasses, was to facilitate movement between VTOL mode, transition mode and conventional (horizontal) flight mode. The diverter unit would effectively direct the exhaust gas flow from the engine aft when in conventional flight. The thrust would be directed forward, via a complex of ducting, to the quad-augmenter complex housed in the wings and canards of the XFV-12A to provision operation of the aircraft in V/STOL modes – the central engine nozzle and 'coanda nozzles' housed on the diffuser flaps directing exhaust gasses into the gaps created by opening the augmenter flaps (coanda jets are integrated into the ejector inlets) (Murphy *et al* c1970's & Culpepper *et al*, 1979 & Bevilaqua & Lee, 1980). This had the effect that the quantity of captured ambient air could equate to several times the engine exhaust mass flow value. The augmenters produced thrust values higher than that produced by the exhaust nozzle due to the fact that engine exhaust kinetic energy was relocated to the captured secondary air (Culpepper *et al*, 1979).

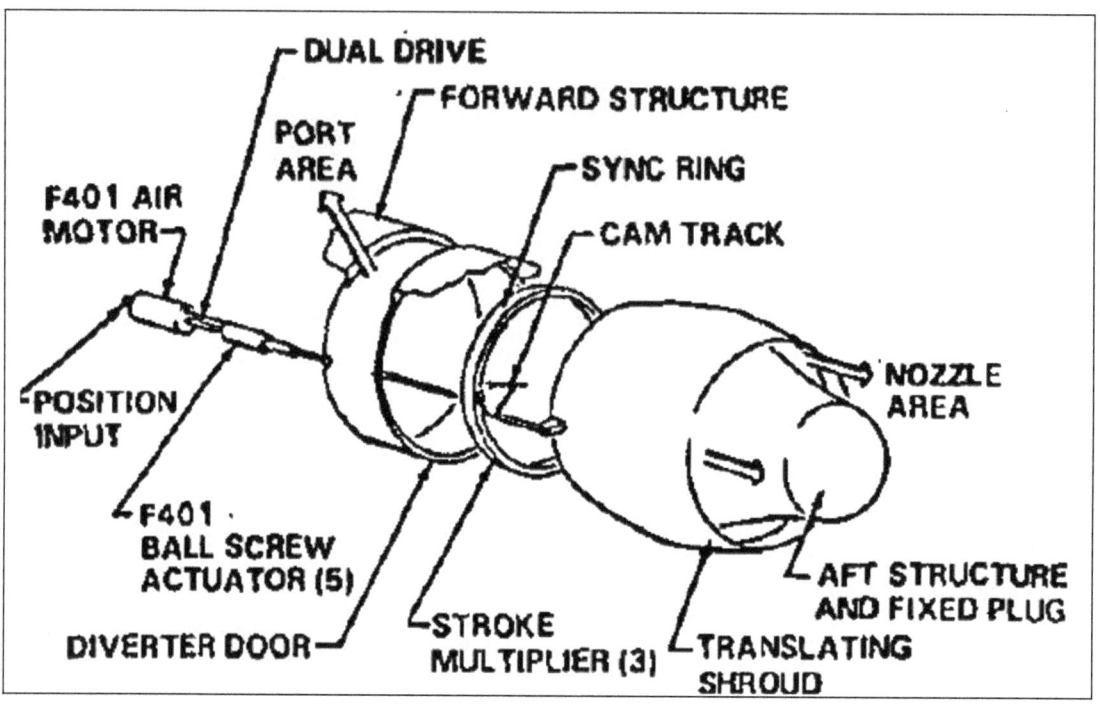

Diagram showing the diverter actuation infrastructure for the diverter intended for the XFV-12A power plant system.

When developing the engine/diverter system a number of basic criteria were laid down along with other areas to be considered:

1. The engine should be capable of operation in the various operating modes with the least possible effect on the engine components and operating idiosyncrasies.
2. The system was not to be over complicated in order to enhance reliability and maintainability.
3. The diverter for the XFV-12A was to be developed without an afterburner function to reduce the development complexity as it was not considered integral to the test of the thrust augmented wing concept, the primary remit of the XFV-12A program.

4. The design would incorporate parts from existing platforms where possible, even if this had the undesirable effect of increasing weight.
5. There was no requirement for incorporation of advanced technology or materials in manufacture, reducing costs.
6. The development schedule was to be compatible with the development schedule for the XFV-12A airframe.
7. Ground based models and full-scale ground testing was to be conducted in order to prove the functionality of the diverter and its compatibility with the YF401-PW-400 turbofan engine (Delany & Jenkins, 1976).

The XFV-12A development aircraft, resplendent in a blue white livery in which it conducted the tethered hover test phases. Note the translating plug nozzle engine exhaust that replaced the conventional exhaust/BBN on the YF401-PW-400 engine. Rockwell International (Boeing)

The diverter unit substituted for the standard YF401-PW-400 engine afterburner section/BBN (Balanced Beam Nozzle) on the standard YF401-PW-400 optimised for conventional flight. Elements of the BBN – air drive motor and actuators – were carried over to the diverter system, which consisted of a number of units:

1. A static structure at the front.
2. An aft static structure, incorporating a fixed plug unit.
3. The diverter door complex, concentric in relation to the forward static complex.
4. The concentric shroud, which is concentric with the rear static complex.
5. The actuation system, incorporating a motor/actuation system to power the doors for the diverter complex.
6. Diverter units, forward and aft.
7. Measures, such as seals, to reduce the volume of leaks when operating in all XFV-12A flight modes (Delany & Jenkins, 1976).

To achieve efficient operation of the engine when operating the ejector, it was concluded that the engine exhaust area should be equal to the fringe of the area of the rear exhaust exit pipe. The value for the XFV-12A YF401 engine exhaust nozzle area/ejector primary nozzle matching area was around 8.3 ft.^{2} (0.77 m^2) (Lowry, c1979 in Lopez *et al*, 1979). Insufficient nozzle area can result in a back pressure phenomena. The resultant adverse effects of a reduction in available engine thrust and excessive area can induce a reduction in the engine stall margins. The design of the ejector system and the determination of nozzle area would be unequivocally linked if efficient operation was to be achieved (Lowry, c1979 in Lopez *et al*, 1979).

During the diverter development phase a one eighth scale model of the diverter was designed, built and tested in order to verify early analytical predictions. The tests resulted in the analytical prediction data being modified prior to design of the full-scale diverter. A full-scale fixed (non-flight rated) diverter was tested by Pratt & Whitney, along with a non-flight rated XF401-PW-400 engine, serial FX212-13. This was primarily to prove functionality and compatibility of the engine/diverter with a secondary objective of verification of data concerning hot gas flow. Both primary and secondary objectives were met. Following these tests the engine and diverter were transported to Rockwell's Columbus Aircraft Division for extensive full-scale ground tests.

A fully operational, flight rated, movable diverter was installed on XF401-PW-400 engine, serial XF210-13, for ground testing on a test stand to investigate the characteristics of engine operation in the various modes – vertical, transition and horizontal. This included garnering data on diverter/engine transition rate effects on engine performance, overall diverter operation, pressure loss and diffusion of heat for correlation with data obtained from laboratory research on hot gas conducted during the fixed diverter development test phase. The results showed that the mechanics of the diverter were at acceptable operation levels and that the diverter operation was superior to that suggested by the data on hot gas and, being on a par with data obtained during the fixed diverter test phase. Values for transition times for the diverter were 1.5 to 10 seconds. There was a problem with unacceptable levels of engine surge when the diverter doors were put into the mid-transition position and during sudden movement of the engine operation from idle to the intermediate setting (Delany & Jenkins, 1976). Although such a scenario would be detrimental to an operational design, it was considered acceptable for the XFV-12A demonstration program as this did not require operation with the diverter door fixed in the mid-position. The problem was further alleviated as a cause of concern, in regard to the XFV-12A, when data obtained from tests employing a flight-rated YF401-PW-400 in place of the experimental XF401-PW-400, were not subjected to the same phenomenon (Delany & Jenkins, 1976).

Page 32-35: XFV-12A airframe assembly/testing at Rockwell International Aircraft Division's Columbus facility on 22 January 1973. Rockwell International (Boeing)

DUCTING SYSTEM – A complex of ducting – runs augmentation bellows rotating vanes, provision for insulation and fixings mounting the components – linked the XFV-12A propulsion system to the ejector system (Lowry, c1979 in Lopez *et al*, 1979). The thin-gauge ducts were manufactured from titanium alloys (Rockwell International XFV-12A D&DP, 1981). As with other elements of the overall augmentation system, the ducting increased aircraft weight (the ducting system installed on the XFV-12A had a weight in the region of 900 lb. (~400 kg)) and overall size and can be the source of thrust loss due to loss of pressure as well as complicating maintenance (Lowry, c1979 in Lopez *et al*, 1979). Incorporation of a ducting system can result in a pre-augmentation thrust loss value in the region of 8%, shown in various calculation models. The actual pre-augmentation pressure loss encountered in the XFV-12A was estimated to be somewhere in the region of 12% (corresponding to around 6% pre-augmentation thrust loss), 2% more pressure loss than that estimated for the XV-4A (Lowry, c1979 in Lopez *et al*, 1979). The less pressure loss in the ducting complex the more thrust reached the augmenter, maximising available lift (Delany & Jenkins, 1976).

AUGMENTERS – Augmenters have the dual role of increasing net thrust and directing thrust in a particular direction to meet a specific purpose – production of lift in the case of the XFV-12A.

Page 36-37: XFV-12A cruise flight wind-tunnel testing, 1974. Force test cruise flights – Test 355 – were conducted in Building 643. NASA

The compound ejector thrust augmenter complex installed in the XFV-12A wings and canards consisted of a family of flaps (each augmenter consisted of a shroud, itself made up of pair of opposed Coanda type slot nozzle flaps along and a nozzle assembly on the central body) that open and close to take advantage of the energy in the engine exhaust. This exhaust was diverted to the augmenter complex through the combined plug nozzle-sleeve valve. It was then passed through ducting to slots positioned on the diffuser entrance sides – the diffuser being formed of the flaps (Throndson, 1973, McCormick, 1970's, Delany & Jenkins, 1976, Rockwell International XFV-12A D&DP, 1981 & Stewart, 1981). Thrust augmentation produced approximately 50% increase in pre-augmentation engine thrust (Leon, 1982).

To achieve vertical flight the augmenters are deflected to maximum downward position and moved toward an angle approaching that of the plane of the wing for conversion to conventional (wing-borne flight).

The degree of thrust augmentation required would be relative to secondary air-flow volume, which could be regulated/varied, through altering the angle of the diffuser flap, with corresponding alterations on the degree of lift thrust generated from each respective augmenter surface (Murphy *et al* c1970's). Through simultaneous varying of the diffuser half-angles (simultaneous variation of the area that air flow exits the augmenter, through altering the angle of the diffuser flaps) – conducted through movement of the lift lever located next to the cockpit throttle controls – on the two wing and two canard mounted augmenters, the pilot can alter the hover altitude without any corresponding increase in engine thrust (Culpepper *et al*, 1979 & Rockwell International XFV-12A D&DP, 1981). In effect, the amount of lift that is generated by each of the four augmenters, and, therefore, the variation of height control, can be varied without increased engine thrust output. This is accomplished through simultaneous variation of the area that air flow exits the augmenter, through altering the angle of the diffuser flaps (Rockwell International XFV-12A D&DP, 1981 & Culpepper *et al*, 1979).

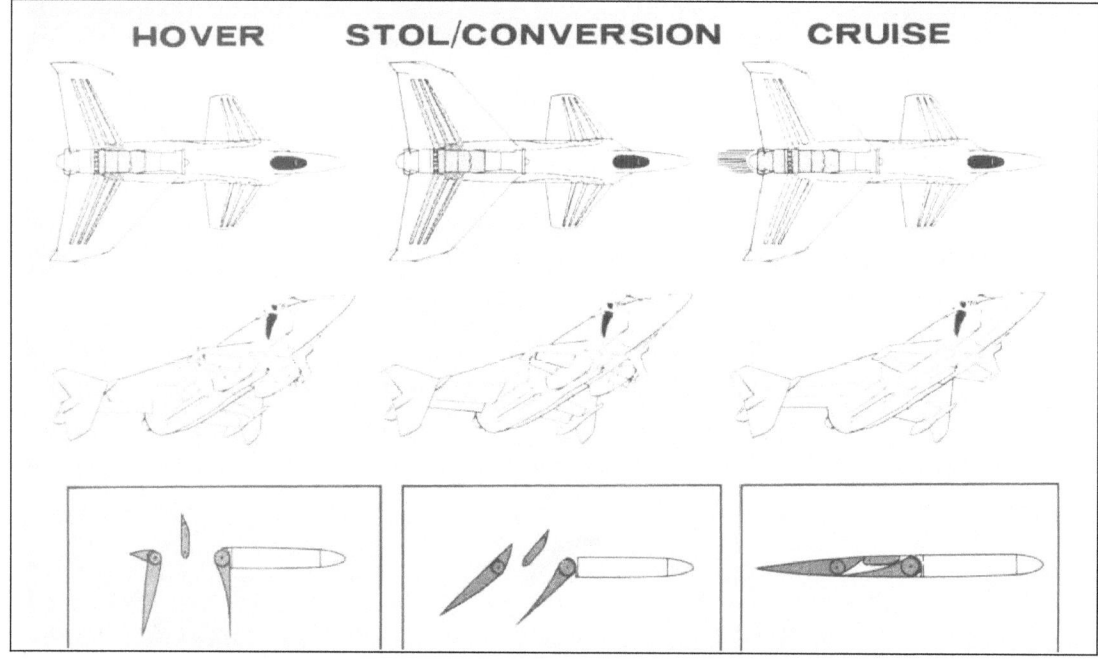

Diagram showing the positioning of the augmenter flaps for the three XFV-12A flight modes – hover, STOL/conversion and cruise. Rockwell International (Boeing)

For climb a lever is moved from neutral to the forward position and moved from neutral to aft for descent. Aircraft attitude control in pitch is accomplished through differential alterations to diffuser half-angles on the wing and canard whilst roll control is achieved through differentially altering the half-angles on each of the wings with differential altering of angles of the flaps on the wing mounted augmenter for control in yaw (Culpepper *et al*, 1979). Controlling aircraft attitude in pitch would be conducted through differential movement, creating differential lift, of the wing and canard mounted diffuser flaps. Controlling attitude in roll was accomplished through differential movement, creating differential lift, of the starboard and port wing mounted diffuser flaps. Yawing movement was achieved through implementing differential average augmenter angles of the starboard and port wings (Murphy *et al* c1970's & Rockwell International XFV-12A D&DP, 1981).

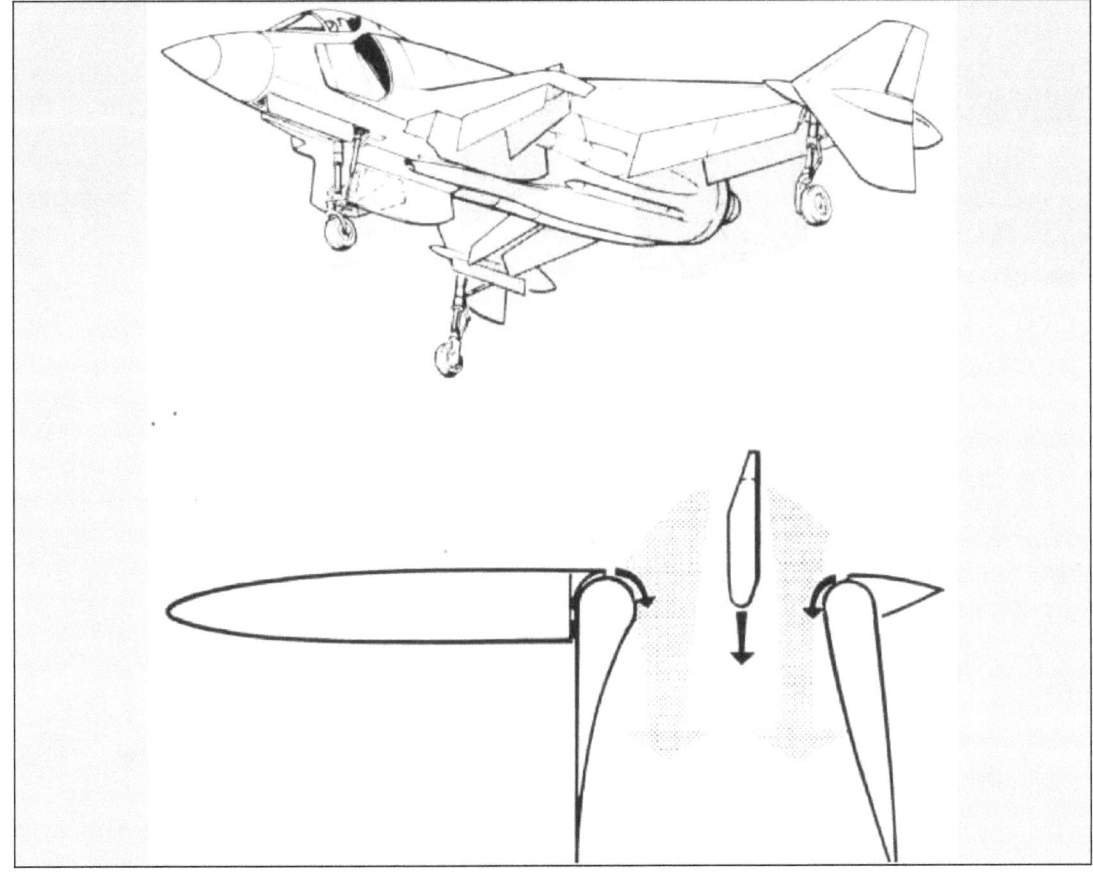

XFV-12A lift TAW concept showing the downward redirection of ducted air to provide lift. North American (Rockwell/Boeing)

When the aircraft was to commence conversion from hovering flight to conventional flight the augmenters forced captured secondary air over the aerodynamic surfaces. This resulted in swift accumulation of lift forces through airflow circulation of wing and canard aerodynamic surfaces (Culpepper *et al*, 1979). The conversion process would result in the augmenter flaps resorting to angles under 30°, through progressive movement from the open to closed configuration (Rockwell International XFV-12A D&DP, 1981). At this point the aircraft would revert back to normal/conventional engine nozzle thrust mode, the augmenter complex – ejector centre structure and flaps – folding away as the aircraft tidied-up to adopt a high performance aerodynamic layout. This involved the trailing-edge flaps, located on the wing and canard surfaces, assuming the role of conventional aerodynamic control surfaces (Culpepper *et al*, 1979). In the transition phase of flight the XFV-12A would receive additional lift through a process – force attributed to a forceful jet flap resulting in super-circulation lift, which was characteristic of the TAW concept (Rockwell International XFV-12A D&DP, 1981).

Once transition was complete, primary gas flow from the engine would be directed rearward through the engine nozzle. With the aircraft now in conventional flight mode the augmenter flaps would be fully retracted, to assume the role of a standard aerofoil section, with the rearmost augmenter flaps on the wings and canards taking on the function of aerodynamic control surfaces as on a CTOL aircraft (noted above) (Rockwell International XFV-12A D&DP, 1981). When the XFV-12A transitioned from VTOL to horizontal flight, the flaps had to be rotated from their conventional flight position, which was a complex operation, but had benefits over previously employed practice. Avoiding the need for doors that would open and close to expose and protect the augmentation system reduced or removed the problem of back pressure, which would incur a loss of thrust output (Lowry, c1979 in Lopez *et al*, 1979).

The aft wing and canard flaps conferred aircraft control in pitch with the wing flaps conferring roll control when employed differentially. A speed brake function was provided by the simultaneous use of the aft and forward wing flaps. Operation of the port and starboard rudders provided control in yaw during conventional flight (Rockwell International XFV-12A D&DP, 1981).

Augmenter testing was conducted with a rectangular augmenter design with a span of 20 in. (~51 cm). This was installed on a test stand powered (producing gas flow) by a modified General Electric J79 turbojet engine as part of an independent research and development effort that determined that the augmenter concept, incorporating a twin Coanda/central body principle, was feasible (Delany & Jenkins, 1976).

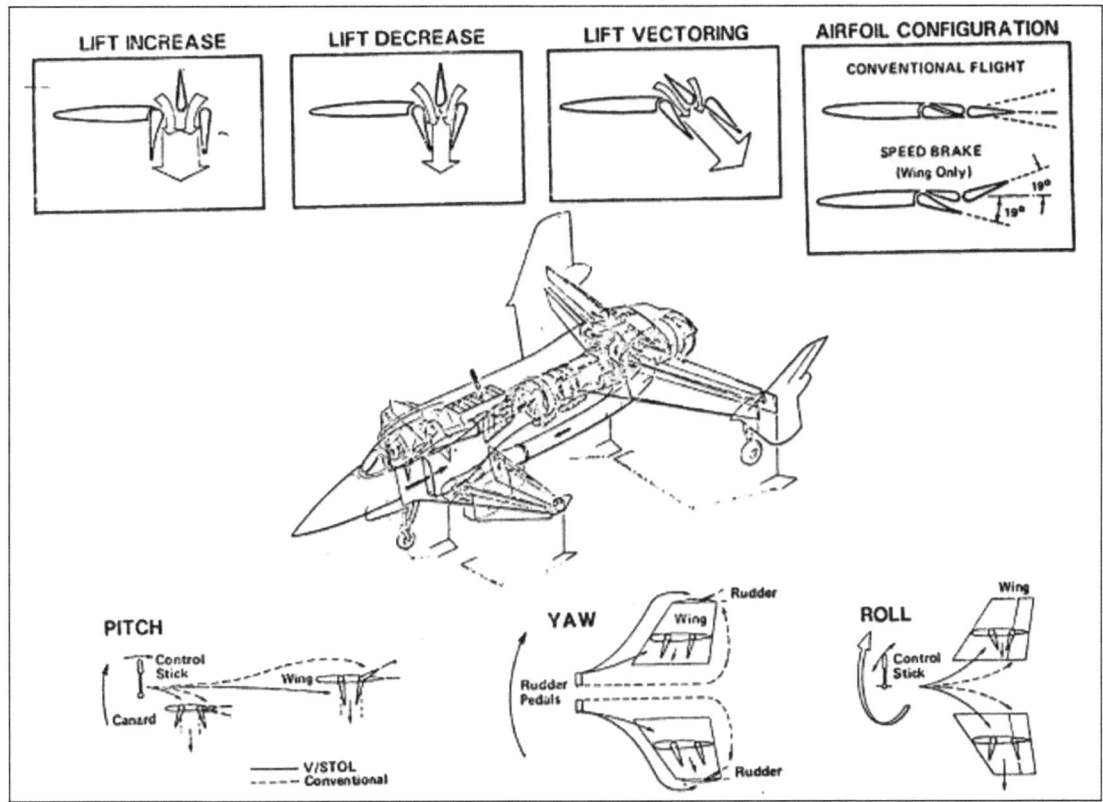

XFV-12A lift and control. Rockwell International (Boeing)

FLIGHT CONTROL – As normal aerodynamic controls lost their effectiveness in extreme low-speed flight and when the aircraft was in hover flight mode the XFV-12A required incorporation of an adscititious control power system. Referred to as a total force management system, this utilised the ejector for provisioning control in pitch, roll, yaw, and altitude and force vector. This required retention of some lift to provision for hover control. Other traits of such a system included reduced lateral control capability at the low-speeds associated with the transition phase when speed is insufficient for aerodynamic control to become effective (Lowry, c1979 in Lopez *et al*, 1979).

Although emphasis was mostly placed on the vertical element of the V/STOL, the XFV-12A would have been able to operate in STOL mode. When operating in STOL mode a jet-flapped type of effect, not dissimilar to that of an externally blown flap effect, would be produced. STOL operations allowed increased weight values for operational load to be carried, typically an increase of up to 5,000 lb. (~2268 kg) compared to that offered by the vertical take-off option when the aircraft conducts a short – 328 ft. (~100 m) – rolling take-off run (NASA Advances in Engineering Science Vol.4, 1976).

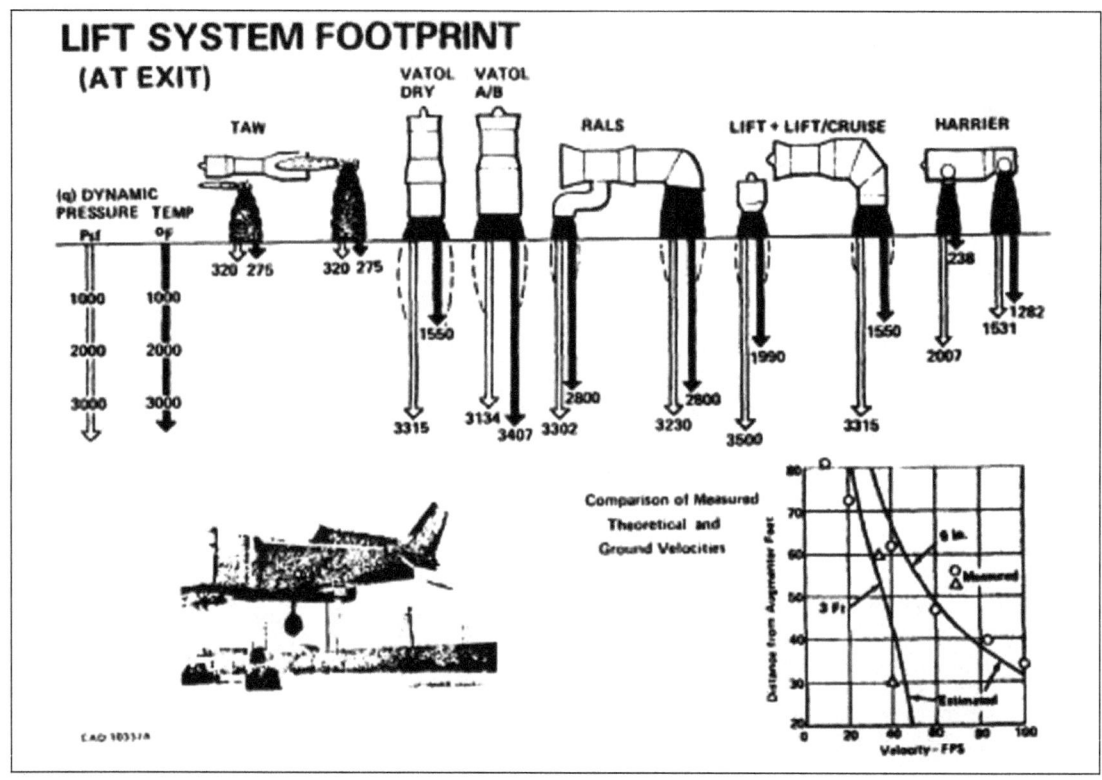

Comparison of the thrust augmented wing (TAW) concept with that of other types of vertical lift clearly showed that TAW offered much reduced surface footprint. Rockwell International (Boeing)

The TAW concept promised significant improvements to the problem of reducing the detrimental effects of V/STOL footprint compared with other concepts, such as direct lift systems. The TAW concept offered solutions to surface erosion problems due to its low operating temperature and low pressure. This was accomplished through the mixing of ambient air, the secondary airflow in significant quantity –

up to several times the value of the primary airflow – which resulted in a reduction of pressure at the exhaust and reduced temperatures at the exit plane of the augmenter to values of 320 psi and 275° F respectively (Rockwell International XFV-12A D&DP, 1981). In other words, air from the engine fan and core were mixed, providing an overall cooling effect before the primary airflow was forced through the four ejectors and cooled further as it contacted the secondary ejector airflow (Luidens *et al*, 1984).

The cool low pressure air flow produced in ground effect was considered a desirable trait, particularly for a naval fighter aircraft designed to operate from the deck of a ship platform. It was also conducive with successful operations from relatively unprepared terrestrial airfields (Leon, 1982). Such operating conditions of pressure and temperature produced in the TAW concept promised to be benign enough for the safe operation of surface personnel in the vicinity of the aircraft, even when it was operating in V/STOL mode (Rockwell International XFV-12A D&DP, 1981).

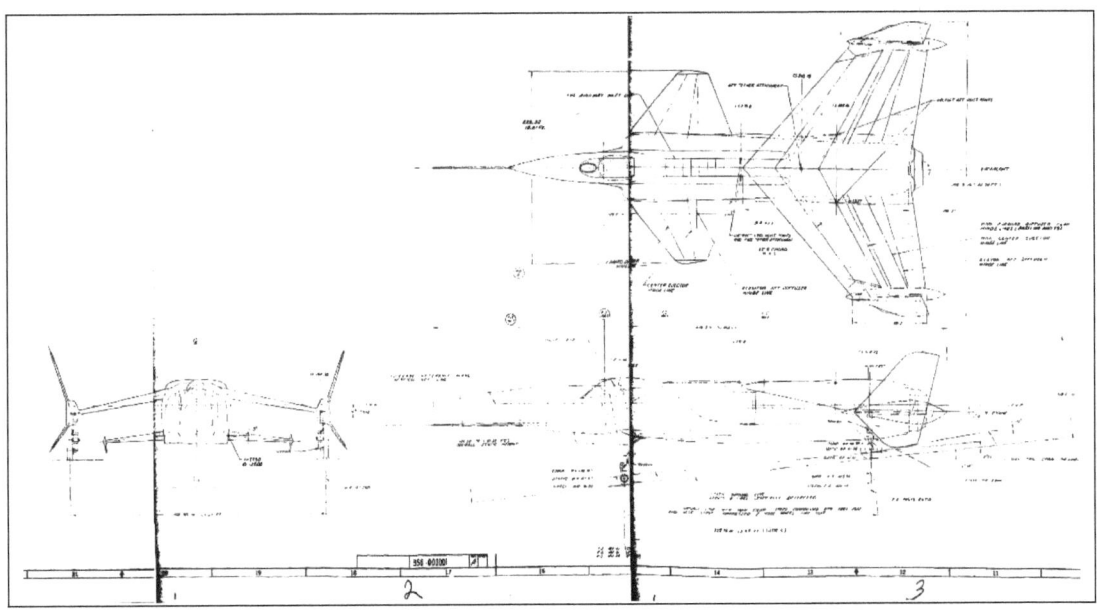

Design office general arrangement of the XFV-12A dated c1974. The text supporting the drawing is mostly illegible, but basically indicates the various design characteristics of the aircraft – air induction system, main wing and canard, along with diffuser flaps and wingtip mounted vertical surfaces. The main purpose of the drawings inclusion is to illustrate the design at a particular stage in the program timeline. Rockwell International (Boeing)

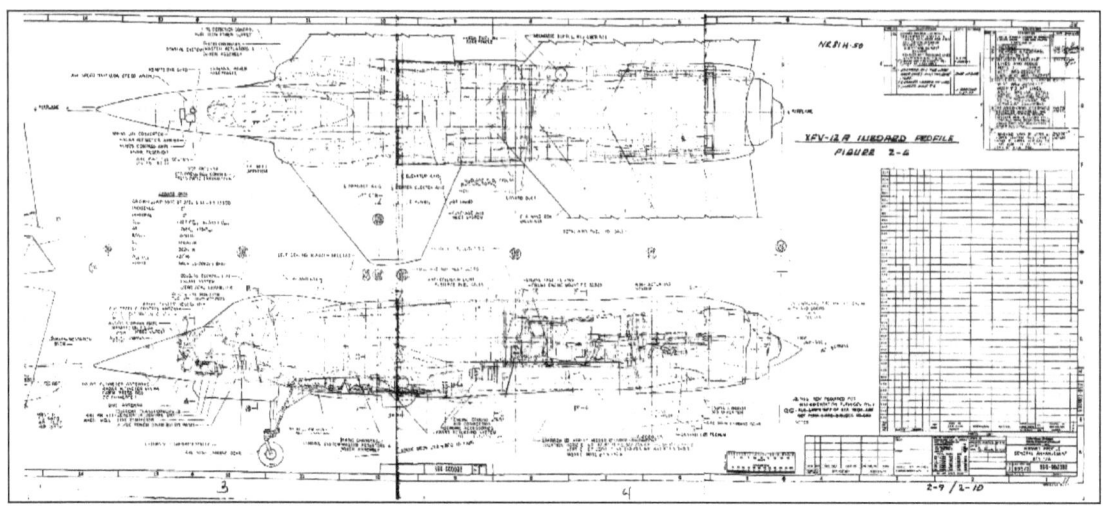

XFV-12A design office drawing dated c1974. The supporting text basically indicates some of the equipment fit intended for the XFV-12A, outlined in the main text below. Rockwell International (Boeing)

Basic equipment and instrumentation included in the XFV-12A design during the 1974-1977 timeframe included the following: Nose section – Air speed unit (low speed V/STOL), ASN/75 DIR Gyro, MB-5A LOX converter, APN-94 radar altimeter, ASN/75 Compass AMPL, Brake reservoir, Air traffic control antenna, Instrumentation boom, Radar altimeter antenna on underside and DC Converter. After nose/cockpit underside – DME Antenna, current transformers, generator control unit, line contractor and AC/DC power distribution panel. Cockpit – VOR Antenna, ECD Press REG control, FRESS Ratio transmitter, Douglas Escapac I AI pilot zero-zero ejection system (deactivated during tethered hover testing), Pilots eye position – FUS STA 111625, WP 2050. External – Fire detection control, Fuel flow power supply, External power receptacle on starboard forward fuselage underside and High Frequency Antenna just aft of the cockpit. After fuselage – engine ground start, air connection and engine accessories (Rockwell International XFV-12A D&DP, 1981).

Although intended for a purely research effort aimed at proving the TAW concept viability for incorporation into a tactical fighter type aircraft, a number of armament options were associated with the XFV-12A. A study conducted at the DTNRSDC (David Taylor Naval Ship Research & Development Center) concluded that in comparison with other V/STOL concepts the TAW had superior load carrying capability,

XFV-12

outperforming L/C (Lift/Cruise) with reaction bleed, L+L/C, (Lift+Lift/Cruise) L/C+Burner (Lift/Cruise+Burner) and Tilt Wing. All concepts were set at a vertical take-off gross weight of 35,000 lb. (~15876 kg), with the aircraft operating from a ship deck on an interception mission (Rockwell International XFV-12A D&DP, 1981).

The most basic armament option was incorporation of an M61A1 multi-barrel 20 mm cannon, apparently on the fuselage starboard underside beneath and aft of the cockpit area (not fitted to the XFV-12A prototype aircraft). Advanced weapon options included the Sparrow III (AIM-7F) semi-active radar homing medium range air to air missile, two of which could be carried semi-recessed on the fuselage underside aft of the canards (the nose section of the missiles protruded beyond the position of the canards). For the air to surface role the aircraft could be armed with two McDonnell Douglas (now Boeing) AGM-84 Harpoon anti-ship missiles, unguided bombs (four MK 82 class) or munitions dispenser. Carriage of each of these weapon options negated the carriage of other weapons options as all were carried on the fuselage underside. Rockwell International artwork indicated the AIM-9 Sidewinder infrared guided short-range air to air missile as an armament option, but it is not clear where these would be accommodated.

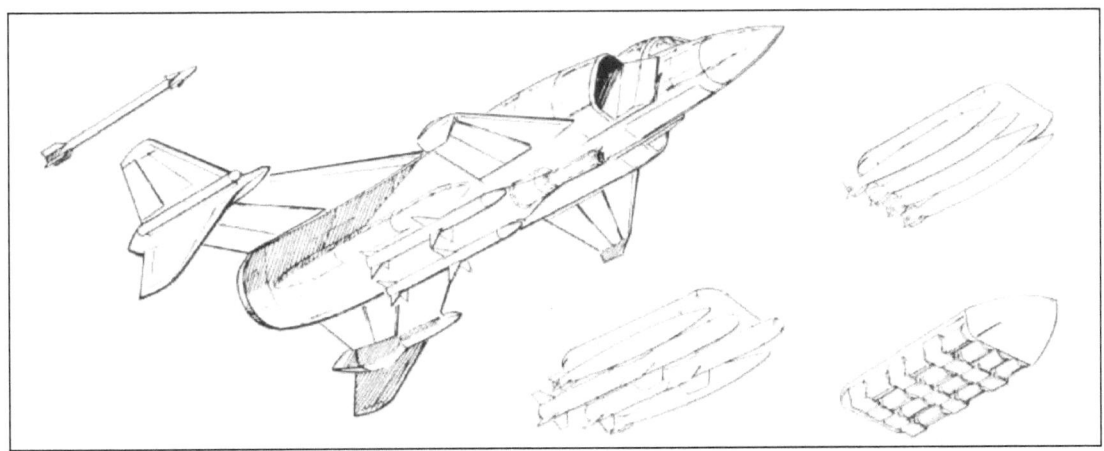

Previous page: Graphic illustration (top) depicting basic armament options for a notional operational variant of the XFV-12A – M61A1 20 mm cannon, unguided bombs and Sparrow III (AIM-7F) semi-active radar homing medium range air to air missiles – and XFV-12A mock-up with AIM-7F incorporated (bottom). This page: XFV-12A mock-up with Sparrow III missiles and 20 mm cannon incorporated. Rockwell International (Boeing).

XFV-12A Characteristics – data from Culpepper *et al*, 1979
Engine: One YF401 turbofan rated at 16,500 lb. (73.4 kN) static-thrust at sea level
Length: 43.9 ft. (13.4 m)
Height: 9.1 ft. (2.8 m)
Main wingspan: 28.5 ft. (8.7 m) and 25.3 ft. (7.7 m)
Gross take-off weight in STOL mode: 25,250 lb. (107.9 kN)
Gross take-off weight in VTOL mode: 19,130 lb. (85.1 kN)
Fuel capacity: 2,040 lb. (9.1 kN) housed in wings and 2,774 lb. (12.3 kN) housed in fuselage for a combined total of 3,014 lb. (21.4 kN)
Moment of inertia in pitch: 51,200 slug-ft^2 (~69407 kg m^2)
Moment of inertia in roll: 13,500 slug-ft^2 (~18303 kg m^2)
Moment of inertia in yaw: 62,800 slug-ft^2 (~85145 kg m^2)

The XFV-12A prototype was rolled-out at Rockwell International's Columbus Aircraft Division, Ohio, on 27 August 1977. The aircraft underwent a series of ground testing before being transferred to NASA Langley Research Center, Virginia, aboard Aero Spacelines Super Guppy transport aircraft in November 1977.

Page 47-48: XFV-12A mock-up. Rockwell International (Boeing)

XFV-12A prototype production line. Only the first development aircraft was completed. Note upward hinged nose section in lower photograph. Boeing

XFV-12A port canard/augmenter complex on the prototype vehicle (top) and the completed vehicle on the ramp at Rockwell's Columbus facility (above). Boeing

2

DEVELOPMENT, STRUCTURAL, FUNCTIONAL, STATIC & DYNAMIC TETHERED HOVER AND DIAGNOSTIC TESTING

The maiden flight of the XFV-12A prototype was initially scheduled for September 1976 (McCormick, 1970's & NASA Advances in Engineering Science Vol.4, 1976). This date is thought to refer to a preliminary schedule for the commencement of tethered hover testing rather than a date for free flight testing. It is often stated that the XFV-12A should have been flown in conventional take-off and landing/cruise flight mode prior to concentration of hover testing, tethered or free. However, it should be noted that the primary remit of the XFV-12A research aircraft program was to demonstrate the viability of the thrust augmented wing concept, which could only be accomplished through hover testing. If the VTOL (Vertical Take-Off and Landing)/hover performance was not sufficient then it would have mattered not if the aircraft had poor, adequate or exceptional conventional flight performance. In the conventional cruise flight mode, a most important area of investigation was that of attaining efficient supersonic flight. This would only have been possible through extensive ground test to clear the unmodified YF401-PW-400 engine for flight in the aircraft, pushing back testing of and clearing the YF401-PW-400 engine modified for V/STOL (Vertical/Short Take-Off and Landing) operations. Such a move would have delayed the tethered hover tests intended to investigate the V/STOL capability of the thrust augmented wing concept, the programs primary remit, as noted above.

Key areas that were to be investigated during the development program included analysis of aerodynamic and propulsive spheres and assessment of the flight qualities of an aircraft configured with a high wing/low canard. Aircraft stability and control whilst in the VTOL and transition from vertical to cruise flight modes was to be investigated. An analysis of the compatibility of the YF401 power plant with the exhaust diverter complex element of the TAW (Thrust Augmented Wing) concept was to be conducted. The efficiency of ducting, through which gas flow would reach the augmenters, was to be analysed and an assessment conducted on whether the designs augmentation ratio was conducive to effective VTOL operation. Of the above research areas to be investigated, only the flight qualities of an aircraft configured with a high wing/low canard was satisfactorily examined during the development phase, the remaining research questions requiring actual flight data for correlation with development data extracted from various scale-model tests, to be satisfactorily answered (Rockwell International XFV-12A D&DP, 1981).

Scale model tests were conducted in the NASA 12 ft. (~3.66 m) low speed wind tunnel during 1973. NASA

XFV-12A scale model undergoing force control testing with **NASA** during **1974.** NASA

The development process included extensive testing of scale models, ground-based simulations and various rigs for testing systems and certain aircraft flight modes. The flight qualities of an aircraft configured with a high wing/low canard layout were extensively researched (see previous section), including a series of high speed wind tunnel tests conducted on a 0.03 scale-model prior to the second half of 1973, and low speed wind tunnel tests conducted on a 0.20 scale-model prior to the second quarter of 1973 (Murphy *et al* c1970's & Reports 73CL 2976, 1973, Report 73CL 2655, 1973 & Report 75CL 2104, 1975).

The whirl rig was employed to conduct practical testing on the augmenter complexes prior to the hover flight phases. Rockwell International (Boeing)

A test complex, referred to as the whirl rig, was utilised to test the XFV-12A wing and canard mounted augmenter complexes (NASA). A series of tests were conducted with a rectangular shape augmenter complex, supplied, via ducting, by hot gas exhaust from two General Electric J85-GE-4A turbojet engines. Testing with the J85 engines, which built on pre-whirl rig test data pertaining to measurement, instrumentation and fabrication methods, was discontinued once an YF401 engine became available for the supply of hot gas exhaust for augmenter testing on the whirl rig (Delany & Jenkins, 1976).

The whirl rig was basically a rotating boom with a test rig at the extension, out beyond 100 ft. (~30.48 m), creating conditions for vertical and longitudinal (on a line, such as a longitude from East to West) (Murphy *et al* c1970's & Delany & Jenkins, 1976). The remotely operated whirl rig augmenter was subjected to jet efflux – hot gas emanating from the YF401-PW-400 (XF401-PW-400) engine and directed to the augmenters via the fixed diverter to a collection point where it was forced through an exit door and/or 32 in [~81 cm] in diameter reservoir piping, travelling through the test structure until it reached the augmenters (Delany & Jenkins, 1976). The whirl rig boom was able to vary altitude above ground in order to provide data on static ground effect. The rig was fitted out with necessary instrumentation for taking data measurements to assess performance and variables, such as aerodynamic flow (Murphy *et al* c1970's & Delany & Jenkins, 1976). Data for the augmenter basic performance in generating lift could be gathered with the whirl rig in a fixed position, whilst assessment of the control characteristics at low speeds was conducted with the rig being rotated through the power of the augmenter system. The addition of a main undercarriage unit facilitated testing of vertical take-off and landing, conversion from hover to conventional flight and short take-off and landing whilst the boom was rotated 360° (Delany & Jenkins, 1976). Into the first quarter of 1976, in excess of 250 engine hours of testing of the fixed augmenter were conducted on the whirl rig, providing data that verified expectations on the performance and endurance of the diverter system (Delany & Jenkins, 1976).

XFV-12A ground test rig. Rockwell International

Further testing of the power plant included ground tests of an YF401-PW-400 engine at Rockwell's Columbus Aircraft Division's engine test facility. This engine was attached to an XFV-12A forward fuselage, complete with primary and auxiliary air inlets. The engine was fitted with a fixed area BBN (Balanced Bean Nozzle). In this configuration it was tested up to intermediate power levels, following which the fixed BBN was replaced with an operational (moving/adjustable) BBN. In this configuration the engine was tested in afterburner mode. The fixed and operational BBN engine tests, amounting to around 20 hour's duration, assessed the engine trim, engine inlet and recovery and inlet distortion characteristics, along with assessing engine/air inlet compatibility (Delany & Jenkins, 1976).

A realm of testing during the conception stage included development of V/STOL associated systems and extensive wind-tunnel and flight testing of a plethora of aerodynamic vehicle configuration scale-models. This progressed as the design was outlined and refined for operation in the initial powered lift, transition from powered lift to forward flight and conventional winged flight modes (Murphy *et al* c1970's).

Assembly of XFV-12A prototype number one was structurally completed in early 1977, paving the way for commencement of functional and structural ground testing. This was conducted at Rockwell International Corporations Columbus Aircraft Division, Ohio, where the aircraft had been built. This phase effectively confirmed the viability of operation of the XFV-12A on-board systems (Rockwell International XFV-12A D&DP, 1981).

A series of critical design condition structural load tests was conducted on the aircraft sections – wing, canard and vertical tail – in order that the basic CTOL (Conventional Take-Off and Landing) flight envelope could be defined. Other ground based testing included vibration tests designed to assist in the analysis of predicted XFV-12A flutter characteristics (Murphy *et al* c1970's & Rockwell International XFV-12A D&DP, 1981), and studies of such areas as diverse as velocity, temperature, noise, air flow re-ingestion, measures reducing instrumentation data and pilot cockpit procedures (Murphy *et al* c1970's).

During engine/ducting/augmenter functional testing, which evaluated the XFV-12A propulsion and control system when operated in the CTOL mode, the aircraft was positioned on a facility featuring a trio of tie down fixings, each of which contained a 'lift and drag load cell' (Murphy *et al* c1970's). Any results obtained were considered provisional as it was accepted that some modifications to the aircraft would most likely have to be made for the optimum lift/control traits to be attained (Murphy *et al* c1970's).

The prototype XFV-12A. Rockwell International (Boeing)

PERFORMANCE and CONTROL TESTING – The testing conducted under the functional test and structural test phases was subjected to a customer (USN – United States Navy) review, which was passed in November 1977 (Murphy *et al* c1970's). This cleared the way for the tethered hover test phases with the IDRF (Impact Dynamic Research Facility) at the NASA (National Aeronautics and Space Administration) Langley Research Centre. The XFV-12A tethered hover tests at the IDRF would be conducted as a collaborative effort by NASA and the USN NASC (Naval Air Systems Command).

XFV-12A prototype. Rockwell International (Boeing)

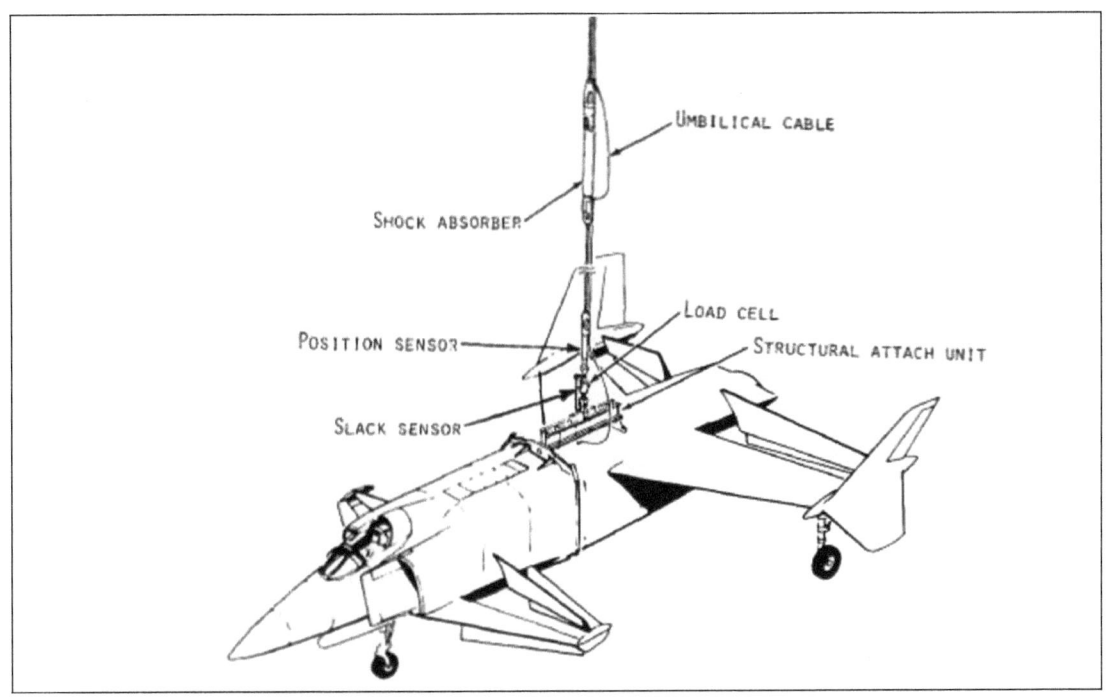

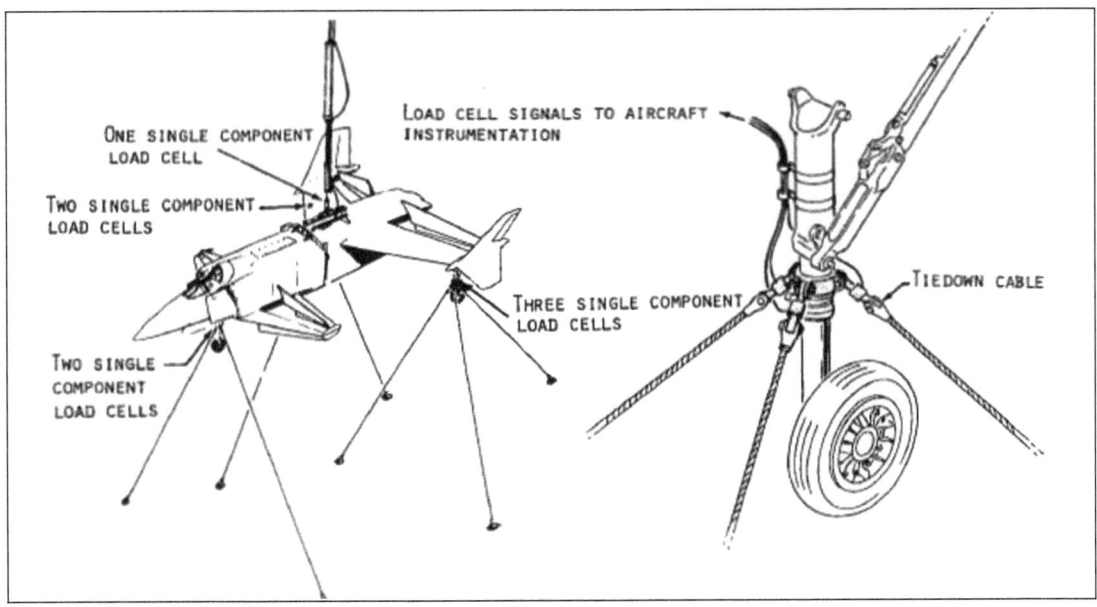

Top: Diagram detailing the lower element of the IDRF 'Z' System. Above: Tie down arrangement for the XFV-12A static hover tests. NASA

Early in the XFV-12A program a study was conducted to find a solution to the requirement for pre-free flight investigation of the completed prototype aircraft characteristics in the hover regime. The use of tethered rigs or pedestal platforms was considered to be inadequate through past experience of other programs leading to inaccurate data about the control response of the air vehicle(s). It was determined that to eliminate or reduce erroneous data in the XFV-12A program that a suitable test facility should be able to allow adequate tests to be conducted to meet a number of objectives. 1. Test the vehicle in hover mode, whilst tethered, at various attitudes and altitudes in order to garner data on force and moment in ground effect and out of ground effect; garner data on the lift and balance traits of the aircraft when operating in ground effect and out of ground effect and provide data on modifications required for the vertical take-off and landing system. 2. Test the aircraft dynamically whilst in the hover mode (limited envelope) to garner data that could be correlated with the results of static tests; garner data on the vehicles responses to control inputs whilst operating in ground effect and out of ground effect and garner data on how ambient wind, including gusts, effect the aircraft in hover. 3. Provide pilot training in vertical take-off and landing mode in as realistic an environment as possible short of actual free flight. 4. Determination of optimum external environmental conditions – noise, temperature, velocity pressure and field of flow – surrounding the vehicle whilst operating in a range of vertical take-off and landing altitude and attitudes in a range of wind strengths (Culpepper *et al*, 1979).

The IDRF was selected as the most suitable existing facility that could be modified to meet the above test objectives, resulting in an agreement being formalised between NASA and NASC (Naval Air Systems Command) late in 1976 for its utilisation in the XFV-12A hover test phase. The IDRF tethered hovering rig was a unique structure that was developed from a USN shipboard underway replenishment variable speed winch (NA Murphy *et al* c1970's SC). The IDRF had its beginnings in the early 1960's when it was developed as the Lunar Landing Research Facility for the NASA Apollo Moon landing program that successfully placed humans on the Moon in July 1969. It had been converted to the IDRF following the end of the Apollo lunar program in the early 1970's, and was utilised in a number of aviation development programs (Murphy *et al* c1970's & Culpepper *et al*, 1979).

The particulars of the IDRF included a hoist for the tether with a 5 ft. (~1.52 m) long 'stroke shock absorber' – forces acting on the tether cables were limited to 40,000 lb/f. (~18144 kg/f)– and a positioning sensor designed to facilitate winch use during dynamic testing (Murphy *et al* c1970's). In order to stop lateral digression, which risked the aircraft striking the structure of the test facility, horizontal attitude cables were positioned around the tether structure at a height of 100 ft. (~30.48 m). Further measures to reduce lateral movement of the aircraft in the initial test phase consisted of placement of a 5 ft. diameter ring structure around the tether (Murphy *et al* c1970's).

Modifications to the IDRF were conducted through 1977 to prepare for XFV-12A testing at the facility, which was now to be conducted by a NASA/NASC/North American Division of Rockwell International Corporation combined test team in the first half 1978 (Culpepper *et al*, 1979). The overall IDRF phase of the program was under the control of the IDRF test director. Although test pilots would be responsible for controlling the aircraft during the hover tests, this was done under the authority of the test director whom the pilots were responsible for reporting to for pre-test briefing and post-test debrief. Other elements of the IDRF test operations included the console operator, test coordinator, safety observers, data observers, NASA safety observer and NASA facility coordinator. Although the test director was in charge of the test operation, the NASA safety observer, being the US government representative, had the authority to order the test director to stop an underway test if he considered it necessary on a safety aspect (Murphy *et al* c1970's & Culpepper *et al*, 1979).

The tethered hover test program had two distinct phases – static testing to investigate the XFV-12A force and moment characteristics and dynamic tests to investigate the hover and control viability of the XFV-12A TAW concept (Rockwell International XFV-12A D&DP, 1981). Lift and moment data was obtained through a grouping of sensor 'load cells' located on the tethers (Murphy *et al* c1970's).

STATIC TESTING – The IDRF facility offered the ability to provision static hover testing of flight vehicles corresponding to all pertinent altitudes and attitudes – in ground effect and out of ground effect – that could be attained by the air vehicle. It also provisioned for testing the ability to conduct analysis of the movements conducted by the larger of the vehicles control surfaces. Another function provided by the facility was to investigate the aircraft hovering envelope. All of the test series provided practical experience for pilot(s) in controlling the aircraft in a variety of environments (Murphy *et al* c1970's).

The XFV-12A underwent a ground test and preparation phase prior to commencement of the static and dynamic hover testing at NASA Langley Research Center. Rockwell International (Boeing)

For the static test phase the XFV-12A, which had been delivered to Langley aboard a Super Guppy transport aircraft in November 1977, was lifted on a tether – the 'Z' system cable – to a predetermined height where it was placed and fixed in a predetermined attitude by seven cables fixed to the ground and extended to attach points on the aircraft undercarriage units. The seven tie-down cables could be adjusted to provision for operations at four test altitudes – 0 ft. (0 m), 3 ft. (~0.9 m), 10 ft. (~3.0 m) and 30 ft. (~9.1 m). Operations at these set altitudes were sufficient for garnering data on the XFV-12A force and moment when operating in ground-effect and out of ground-effect (Murphy *et al* c1970's & Culpepper *et al*, 1979).

The XFV-12A air vehicle and the IDRF facility underwent pre-test inspection. That, for the former, was akin to pre-flight procedures for an actual free flight test. Following pre-test inspection the XFV-12A prototype vehicle was moved into position and the various ground support equipment was installed – this included being connected to a ground based electric power source. A pre-test briefing covered test objectives, aircraft status and configuration and, for subsequent tests following the initial test, a review of any problems encountered during the previous test and fixes introduced. The briefing concluded and a Tether Test Operational Readiness Report was signed by the key members of the test team. Ground support and safety assets were put in place, such as fire and rescue units. Once the various test facilities, including control rooms, were secured the aircraft was lifted off the ground to 1 ft. (~0.3 m) and weighed before being hoisted into position for commencement of the test point. For the static tests the aircraft attitude was altered through adjusters on the seven cables fixing the aircraft in place. Once the aircraft was secured at the required altitude and attitude, engine start-up was conducted by a cable measuring 30.48 m (~100 ft.), this being removed once engine start was accomplished. Following completion of the test point, engine shutdown occurred whilst the aircraft remained in the static tethered position, following which the aircraft was brought to ground level. A post-flight briefing covered preliminary test data, including results and any abnormal issues that may have occurred. The aircraft was put through a post-flight inspection and then prepared for future test operations (Culpepper *et al*, 1979).

The goal of the IDRF static hover tests was to gain maximum development of the XFV-12A augmenters; provision of an evaluation phase of the aircraft stability and control characteristics; provision of data on external forces interacting with the aircraft, both in ground-effect and out of ground-effect, and to assess the integrity of the XFV-12A ducting/augmenter complexes (Murphy *et al* c1970's).

After the static testing got underway it became apparent that the calculated lift of the XFV-12A design was less than had been forecast. The tethered test program had to be reassessed, resulting in three additional test objectives being included. 1. To carry on with as much of the static test program as was possible, with the limitations that would now be inherent due to the deficiency in lift capability. 2. Locate and investigate the reason(s) behind the lower than forecast lift capability through a series of diagnostic tests. 3. Based on diagnostic data obtained, investigate the viability of introducing improvements to increase augmenter system performance – this latter point was a major research goal for the static testing. The additional testing meant the tethered hover test phases – static and dynamic – were increased in duration from the originally planned 12 weeks to 26 weeks, more than double the original time allocated (Rockwell International XFV-12A D&DP, 1981).

In the initial stage of static testing, the focus was put on evaluating the effects of single-axis control commands only. Other areas investigated included the problems of control hysteresis on the diffuser flap angles – 2° for the wing flaps and 1° for the canard flaps. Investigation of several multi-input combinations were conducted without revealing significant moment value or control reversal problems (Culpepper *et al*, 1979).

The XFV-12A prototype vehicle during a static tethered hover test run at the IDRF. Rockwell International (Boeing)

During static tests high power engine runs were typically 5-8 minutes in duration, although longer runs were required under certain conditions to ensure reliable data. It was concluded that very little pilot tasking was required during static tests. Initial tests showed pilot workload was dominated by operation of throttle, lift lever, stick and rudder. This resulted in the establishment of the test coordinator post in the IDRF control room with the function of timing the test point being conducted and to provide confirmation of 'pilot control position movements' (Culpepper *et al*, 1979).

The initial test results from the static tethered hover testing showed the augmenter designs were performing at a standard near to the desired augmentation ratios. On the negative side, the augmentation ratios, which had been determined through load cell data, showed under performance, resulting in the modifications to test points noted above. This variation in performance was noted to occur over the full range of altitudes tested from 0 ft. up to 30 ft., resulting in considerable effort being expended by the test team to investigate the abnormality. It was found that if loads were generated into the tether mechanically and then a comparison was made with previously determined data from results of decreased information on load cells, then static confirmation of load measurements was possible. Instrumentation fitted on the aircraft showed that external forces could not be determined with any degree of certainty when compared with laboratory data, with the exception that such forces tended to produce a minor download effect on the airframe at altitudes of 30 ft. (~9.1 m) (Murphy *et al* c1970's).

Analysis of the results of the static tests by the USN and NASA concluded that a dynamic test should be conducted with the lower tether cables absent and the XFV-12A suspended from the rig safety cable when operating at a lift-to-weight ratio under 1. This, it was concluded, would enable assessment of the quality of the aircraft control characteristics a quantitative measurement of the lift for the aircraft formulated on a single load cell, which would provide validation of lift measurements. The new series of tethered hover tests – dynamic test phase – without the lower tester constraints was conducted on 12-14 June 1978, demonstrating the required aircraft attitude controllability and confirming acceptable operability of the aircraft lift system (Murphy *et al* c1970's).

DYNAMIC TEST – The goal for the dynamic test phase was to confirm the vertical control and attitude for the XFV-12A when operating both in ground-effect and out of ground-effect. Removal of the undercarriage tether cables would allow the XFV-12A to be maneuverer within the confines of the facilities infrastructure and remaining constraints described above (Murphy *et al* c1970's & Culpepper *et al*, 1979). The operating envelope measured 50 ft. x 50 ft.

(~15.24 m x ~15.24 m) at ground-level, narrowing to 38 ft. x 38 ft. (~11.6 m x ~11.6 m) at an altitude of 50 ft. (Culpepper *et al*, 1979).

The major difference in initial flight procedures for the dynamic tests concerned the engine start-up, which occurred with the aircraft on the ground, following the initial lift to around 1 ft. altitude for weighing. Once engine start-up was effected, the starter cable and umbilical's, linking the aircraft to ground electrical sources, were removed. When the aircraft was lifted to various altitudes, up to 50 ft., the engine was set at idle. Once at the test altitude the engine thrust was increased in-line with test requirements. For a vertical take-off the engine thrust was increased from ground-level and the aircraft lifted off the ground and rose to the altitude set for the test. The aircraft could be landed vertically under power or with the engine set at idle and the aircraft lowered to the ground by the 'Z' cable, which was attached to a point above the XFV-12A centre of gravity (Culpepper *et al*, 1979).

Dynamic testing focused on investigating the XFV-12A controllability when operating at a lift-to-weight ratio that did not exceed a value of 1. When the lift to weight exceeded a ratio of 1, sensors within the XFV-12A test complex transferred a signal to the winch to begin tracking the XFV-12A's vertical velocity in order to reduce the force effects of the tethers on the landing qualities of the aircraft (Murphy *et al* c1970's & Culpepper *et al*, 1979). The majority of test functions were conducted with the aircraft operating at a lift-to-weight ratio of 0.75, providing a trimmed platform that displayed satisfactory controllability (Culpepper *et al*, 1979). Although the seven grounded tethers were removed, the aircraft was still subjected to tension forces from the 'Z' cable, meaning that the dynamic hover tests would generate data not necessarily conducive with that which would be acquired in a true untethered free hover test. Despite this anomaly the dynamic hover testing provided sufficient qualitative assessment of the XFV-12A handling qualities. This was accomplished when the 'Z' cable was in a near vertical attitude and only marginal pitch and roll angles were present (Culpepper *et al*, 1979).

The three-axis damper augmenter system of the XFV-12A, which had 10% authority, was evaluated out of ground effect with the aircraft operating at maximum thrust at an altitude of 30 ft. (~9.14 m). It was found that the effect of the damper was minimal in regard to the pitch axis, but was slightly more pronounced in regard to the yaw axis and had a significantly increased effect in the roll axis (Culpepper *et al*, 1979).

XFV-12A prototype vehicle suspended from the IDRF complex gantry during the dynamic hover test phase in June 1978, on the occasion of a high level visit of a group of USN Admirals. NASA L-78-4177

The XFV-12A prototype vehicle undergoing a dynamic hover test run at Langley Research Center IDRF. NASA

The dynamic testing included evaluation of two significant pilot workload tasks. 1. Stabilisation of the XFV-12A at an altitude of 30 ft. to 40 ft. (~9.14 m to ~12.2 m) and then conduct a controlled descent into the ground-effect at approximately 10 ft. (~3 m) altitude. 2. Stabilisation of the XFV-12A at an a altitude of 30 ft. with the lift lever in the aft position before being put into the neutral (forward) position) (Culpepper *et al*, 1979). Due to the under-performance of the augmenters (the augmenters did not meet the design performance goals as noted in the static test phase) this effectively resulted in a flattening out of diffuser half-angles, away from more a or less straight position on augmenter lift-curve slope as the aircraft approached the stall. This significantly reduced available control margins (Culpepper *et al*, 1979). Overall results of these tests showed a significant increase in pilot workload when the lift lever was moved near to the neutral stetting. Pilot tasking during the dynamic tests was similar to that expected of an actual free hover test, in stark contrast to the pilot tasks in the static tests, which was akin to that of overseeing cockpit control functions. This is described in basic terms as the pilot being, for the most part, in the head-down attitude during static tests and predominantly in the heads-up attitude during dynamic tests to facilitate observation outside the cockpit, which was required in order to exert control over the dynamic motion of the airframe within the confines of the test facility (Culpepper *et al*, 1979). Overall it was concluded by the test pilots that pilot workload for both static and dynamic tethered-hover tests was within acceptable limits (Rockwell International XFV-12A D&DP, 1981).

The initial dynamic tests were conducted at a wheel level altitude of ~9.1 m and head level altitude of ~12.2 m (this was the altitude that the majority of static hover tests were conducted). A number of problems were encountered in collecting accurate data due to problems in achieving acceptable attitude control due to the presence of the 5 ft. (~1.52 m) restraint ring. This was removed when efficiency in gaining attitude control had been proven, subsequent tests being conducted with only the 'Z' cable restraint, at altitudes ranging from 40 ft. (~12.2 m) down to 10 ft. (~3.0 m) (Culpepper *et al*, 1979).

Through various measures the XFV-12A was able to be precisely maneuverer laterally ±10 ft. (±~3 m) with ease, within the confines of the test structure without making contact with said structure. Sufficient evaluation of the quality of the XFV-12A handling characteristics in the longitudinal and lateral regimes could be conducted only when the 'Z' cable was in an almost vertical attitude and only minor alterations to pitch and roll were present (Culpepper *et al*, 1979).

OVERALL RESULTS – The tethered hover test phases at Langley answered many questions satisfactorily, but ended with additional questions for facets of the design concept. In both static and dynamic test phases a battery of sensors/instrumentation provided telemetry on such areas as temperature, system performance and aircraft loads, for collection by the test team. As a whole the basic thrust augmented wing concept was confirmed as valid during the static hovering tests, along with quantification of the characteristics of the aircraft propulsion. It was found that augmentation ratios for both wing and canard mounted augmenters were considerably below the design goal values (noted above) (Murphy *et al* c1970's). When the static and dynamic test results were compared under identical operating conditions – aircraft trim and power optimised for facilitating the control system functioning inside the more or less straight position on augmenter lift-curve slope, which allowed for extremely precise control of the test aircraft during dynamic testing – the consensus was that they confirmed the viability of the XFV-12A lift system (Murphy *et al* c1970's).

XFV-12A prototype vehicle during the dynamic hover test phase. Boeing

Following the initial research phase a test point conducted was that of investigation of elevated lift with reduced authority over aircraft control through activating a specific 'trim point' that facilitated operation of the aircraft control system 'in the non-linear [not straight on a line] range of the augmenter lift curve slope' (Murphy *et al* c1970's). Although control of the aircraft was considered adequate, it was determined that the work load of the pilot was considerably higher in such an operating environment (Murphy *et al* c1970's).

There were two distinct value sets for total engine run time in vertical take-off and landing mode (tethered). 1. In the region of 46 hours (7.5 hours run time was at intermediate power ratings) (Murphy *et al* c1970's). 2. 28.77 hours (5.36 hours of this time was conducted with the engine at the intermediate power setting) (Rockwell International XFV-12A D&DP, 1981). The engine was noted to have performed more or less in line with pre-test assumptions. Although the integrity of the ducting system structure was noted to have been exceptional, there were some notable problems encountered, including a number of failures of the 'internal vane' and a tear occurred in an 'end wall blowing plenum' – boundary layer separation (Murphy *et al* c1970's & Lopez *et al*, 1979).

There were no serious technical issues reported for the diverter system and the air induction system was noted to have performed satisfactorily. The value obtained for pressure recovery was 97.5%, with only a low level of low-pressure distortion. Measurements of thrust loss during tethered tests showed a value 12.9%, all but 3% of which was attributed to complete loss of pressure, the balance being attributed to loss through leakage. The static & dynamic tethered hover test phases indicated that all in all the propulsion system operated relatively efficiently, favourably addressing the question of YF401 engine/exhaust diverter system compatibility (Rockwell International XFV-12A D&DP, 1981).

Notwithstanding subtle differences, the results of the dynamic hover testing indicated that the XFV-12A control in VTOL mode was comparable to results obtained in pre-tethered hover simulations and simultaneous power requirements set down by Naval Air Systems Command. These results determined that the handling qualities of the XFV-12A in VTOL mode were considered to be acceptable, the high responsiveness of the control system going some way to addressing the investigation of the aircraft stability and control characteristics in the VTOL mode (Rockwell International XFV-12A D&DP, 1981).

During the static and dynamic hover test phases the XFV-12A suffered only minor structural issues, none of which caused notable damage to the actual structure of the aircraft (Rockwell International XFV-12A D&DP, 1981). There was one notable incident when attitude control was lost early in the dynamic test phase, resulting in the test being aborted. The aircraft was safely recovered without any notable detrimental effects (Culpepper *et al*, 1979).

GROUND EFFECTS – The promise of a relatively benign ground (surface) effects footprint in VTOL mode was a major operational advantage promised by the thrust augmented wing concept. Reference to ground effects characteristics of a VTOL aircraft generally refers to four major areas: re-ingestion of hot gasses back into the engine; positive lift (suck-down effects); temperature effects and ground erosion. Test results confirmed that the thrust-augmentation concept was endowed with generally acceptable results in regard to temperature effects and ground erosion effects (based on limited research results), but generally unacceptable performance in regard to hot gas re-ingestion and positive lift (suck-down effects) – caused by excessive airflow coming through the ejector. Hot gas re-ingestion resulted in two major problems. Prominent was a reduction in thrust due to temperature increasing, around 25° F in the XFV-12A, corresponding to a thrust loss of about 5% (a 1% thrust loss could be expected for every 5° F increase in temperature) when operated in ground-effect for short periods. A surge of hot gas that was re-ingested could also result in compressor stall, which, in extreme cases, could result in an engine flame-out (Lowry, c1979 in Lopez *et al*, 1979).

The tethered hover testing provided considerable data that largely confirmed that the TAW concepts promised benign ground-effect footprint could be achieved in practice. The recorded augmenter exhaust temperatures and horizontal velocities at ground level were in the region of 250° F and 6 ft./s to 100 ft./s (~1.82 ft./s to ~30.48 m/s) respectively. The benign nature of the XFV-12A footprint was further evinced through reports from ground personal at the IDRF, further reinforcing the concepts suitability for operations from a surface ship deck (Rockwell International XFV-12A D&DP, 1981).

The aircraft operating characteristics in ground effect were largely in line with data garnered from scale model testing during the development phase. These indicated that the design showed good characteristics in ground effect at all altitudes tested (Rockwell International XFV-12A D&DP, 1981). Results from tethered hover testing indicated that the XFV-12A design would not incur significant reduction in performance as a result of re-ingestion of jet efflux in an operational environment (Rockwell International XFV-12A D&DP, 1981). Post-test results indicated that only a small amount of re-ingestion encountered had occurred through the upper fuselage air inlet (Leon, 1982).

3

DIAGNOSTIC & REDEVELOPMENT PHASES – XFV-12B/C

Following completion of tethered static and dynamic hover testing the XFV-12 program continued with post tether test diagnostic phases, lasting from May 1979 through to June 1981.

The augmenters were isolated for evaluation, the first such tasking, which utilised the whirl rig facility, being applied to the port side wing augmenter complex. The augmenter and associated ducting components were evaluated in an environment where the fuselage, wing leading edge and diverter were simulated. In addition, 'cold flow isolated component testing', conducted in a thermodynamics laboratory, covered the following areas – '(forward diffuser (forward coanda diffuser flap component); elevon (aft coanda diffuser flap component); seven degree hypermixing center-body segment model; inboard and outboard end-wall blowing nozzle assemblies; forward diffuser flap (forward diffuser); aft diffuser (elevon)' and 'center-body (seven degree hypermixing nozzle and plenum assembly)' (Rockwell International XFV-12A D&DP, 1981).

The testing of the port wing augmenter complex confirmed an augmentation ratio (lift/isentropic thrust) value of 1.26 for the wing augmenter system, in line with values obtained during tethered hover test at the IDRF (Impact Dynamic Research Facility). Isolating the augmenters allowed problems to be better identified. Testing on the wing augmenter system revealed excessive span-wise flow angularity, sporadic span-wise distribution of nozzle exit exhaust pressure and lower than predicted thrust coefficient in the aft diffuser flap (elevon). Testing on the forward diffuser flap (forward diffuser) revealed problems of sporadic span-wise distribution of pressure and pressure and temperature induced nozzle gapping. Tests on the central body revealed sporadic span-wise distribution of pressure exiting the nozzle and prodigious flow angularity, whereby the direction of flow over the end-wall is not uniform. End-wall blowing nozzle testing revealed sporadic distribution of pressure exiting the nozzle and prodigious flow angularity, with misdirected flow (Rockwell International XFV-12A D&DP, 1981).

A program of wing augmenter diagnostic testing was conducted. This confirmed that the target performance value of 1.50 and 1.30 augmentation ratio (lift/isentropic thrust), for the wing and canard augmenters respectively, had not been attained during the tethered hover tests at Langley. In regard to the wing augmenters, a target performance value of 1.26 was attained, whilst a value of 1.11 was attained by the canard augmenters. The performance shortfall was attributed to a number of factors, the diagnostic tests suggesting that some of the problems were not merely attributed to the configuration of the augmenter system, but may have been caused by interface problems with the ducting feeding the augmenter system. It was concluded that interface problems had a detrimental effect on the isolated performance and flow quality of the primary augmenter nozzles, with the net effect that augmentation was reduced below the values that had been predicted (Rockwell International XFV-12A D&DP, 1981). It was clear from the tethered hover test results that further investigation into the augmenters underperformance was required in order to find solutions to the goal of increasing performance to an acceptable level.

Following the diagnostic test phase the program entered a research phase intended to address the issues arising from previous test phases. Among the primary focus areas of this phase was enhancement of the augmenter system performance – searching for fixes to the problem of insufficient air flow that had been confirmed during the diagnostic phase, with the aim of implementing any fixes aimed at improving performance. The basic work was to develop an augmenter system with enhanced performance over that fitted in the XFV-12A during the tethered hover testing, commencing with the wing augmenter design, followed by the canard augmenter design. If the desired performance values could be attained the new program called for re-assembly of the XFV-12A prototype aircraft with the new augmenter design installed to undergo a new VTOL (Vertical Take-Off and Landing)/hover test program. Analytical tools were to be improved; scale model testing would be conducted with a focus on finding solutions(s) to the insufficient airflow in the ducting feeding the augmenter; scale-model testing of redesigned augmenter system to allow calculation of potential design augmentation ratio values and a series of studies would assess redesigned augmenter candidates compatibility with available space constraints inherent in the existing XFV-12A design (Rockwell International XFV-12A D&DP, 1981).

The redevelopment phase included a battery of scale model tests/wind tunnel tests that continued during 1981, the year the program was cancelled. NASA, 1981

Improvements were achieved in the performance characteristics of the augmenter system and nozzle section, demonstrated on a 0.20 scale-model that demonstrated an increase in augmentation ratio (lift/isentropic thrust) from the value achieved in the Langley hover testing to 1.64, a value representative of that attained by the wing augmenter in the 0.20 scale-model (Rockwell International XFV-12A D&DP, 1981 & Schum & DeHart, undated), which was still below the predictions ratio ranges of 1.6 up to 2.0 achieved in laboratory research under static conditions (Stewart, 1981). On the whole, research into thrust augmentation proved to be more successful under laboratory conditions than when applied to an actual air vehicle. Laboratory experiments, at times, produced thrust augmentation ratios that exceeded 2. This was considerably in excess of the more modest ratio goal of 1.41 planned for the Lockheed XV-4A and a ratio of 1.55 planned for the XFV-12A. Just as the XV-4A failed to achieve the ratio of 1.41, the XFV-12A failed to achieve the ratio of 1.55. Among the reasons that the XFV-12A, like the XV-4A before it, failed to achieve the design thrust augmentation ratio was inefficiencies in the design of the ejector interface (Lowry, c1979 in Lopez *et al*, 1979).

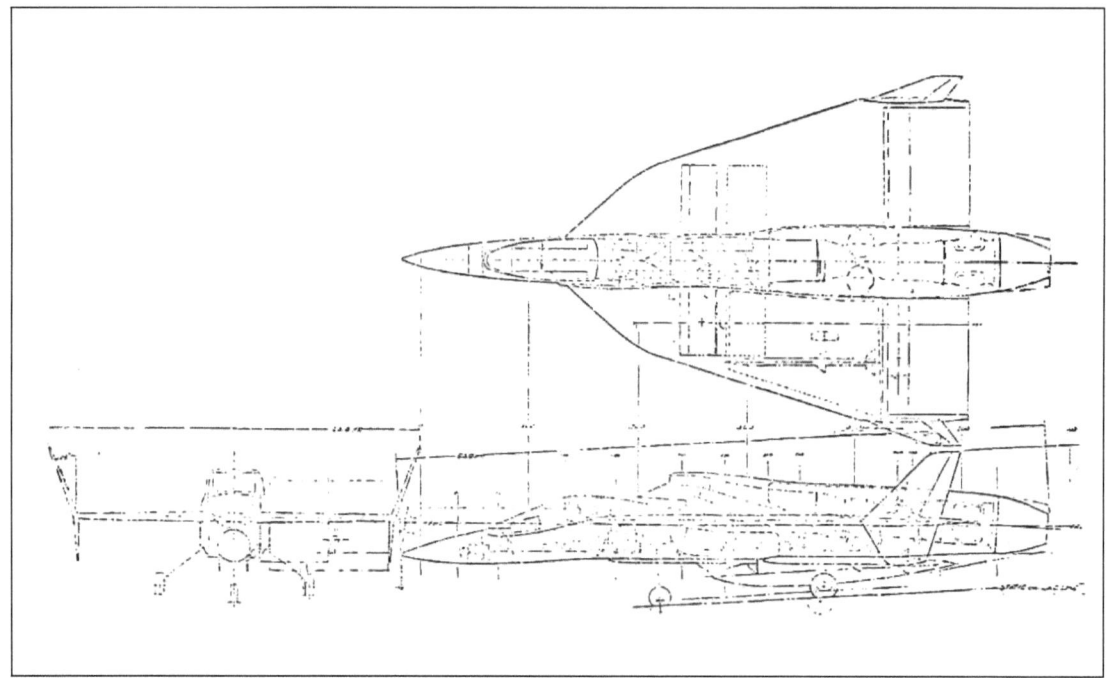

General arrangement drawing of the XFV-12B incorporating the co-planner wing and canard configuration and the fuselage top mounted primary air induction intake. Rockwell International (Boeing)

Whilst the XFV-12A had been developed as a purely research aircraft, concurrent studies were conducted into potential operational configurations of a fighter design employing the thrust augmented wing concept. These emerged as the Rockwell International XFV-12B and XFV-12C. The first of these configurations to be studied was the XFV-12B, which emerged with a blended wing body, referred to as the co-planner wing and canard configuration. Among the most pronounced changes from the XFV-12A was the incorporation of an upper fuselage mounted primary air intake system (Rockwell International XFV-12A D&DP, 1981). Such configurations had been studied in the private sector and by NASA (National Aeronautics and Space Administration) and had been flight tested on the North American YF-107 prototype aircraft, itself an evolution of the North American F-100 Super Sabre series jet powered fighter aircraft. In the mid-late 1970's, Northrop was studying a V/STOL (Vertical/Short Take-Off and Landing) concept featuring an upper intake configuration known as the Vertical Attitude Concept (Gerhardt, & Chen, 1978). In the XFV-12B, the undercarriage system was completely incorporated in the fuselage, a pronounced move away from the wingtip pod mounted main undercarriage units in the XFV-12A. The blended wing, along with other design traits, which would result in reduced supersonic wave drag, were expected to bestow upon the XFV-12B enhanced performance. A major enhancement to the designs vertical lift performance was expected to be inherent in the move to rectangular shaped augmenters, which replaced the swept and tapered augmenters that had been introduced on the XFV-12A. Research efforts had demonstrated that swept and tapered augmenters performed to a lower level than the rectangular augmenters due to problems with span-wise flow resulting from the length of the tapered augmenter flap (Rockwell International XFV-12A D&DP, 1981).

There were musings at the idea of converting the XFV-12A prototype aircraft to XFV-12B standard, resulting in a formal design study to determine such a programs feasibility. It was determined that, just as the XFV-12A had utilised existing components of various aircraft designs, the XFV-12B configuration would utilise components from the XFV-12A where appropriate in order to reduce costs. It was desired to retain the XFV-12A fuselage to wing attachment structure. The span of the aft wing section was increased in order to meet the desired longitudinal stability requirement. Positioning the main undercarriage units on the main wing box structure had the effect that wing anhedral was reduced by a value of 2.0°. Although the XFV-12B design envisioned use of essentially the same diverter system as used on the XFV-12A, the ducting was, for the most part, changed to a simpler arrangement of lighter, less expensive, circular ducts (Rockwell International XFV-12A D&DP, 1981).

The XFV-12B design had a stated operational empty weight of 17,087 lb. (~7751 kg). Gross take-off weight (vertical take-off) was put at

20,476 lb. (~9288 kg), which included a lift reserve of 1,221 lb. (~508 kg). Such weights provisioned for in excess of 15 minutes duration in a vertical hover with the engine at intermediate power setting. This was around twice the hover time available to the XFV-12A (Rockwell International XFV-12A D&DP, 1981).

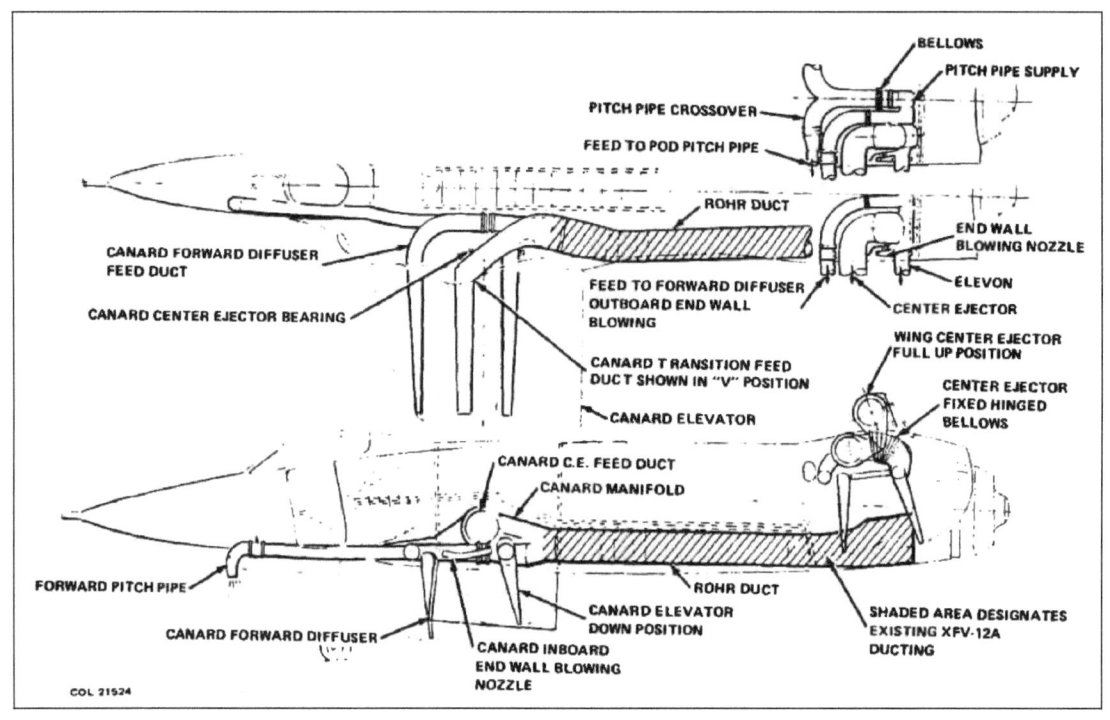

Diagram showing the ducting system of the XFV-12C, highlighting that it is mostly unchanged from that of the XFV-12A. Rockwell International (Boeing)

Cost considerations, as well as technical concerns in such areas as the performance of the XFV-12B blended wing when in the transition phase of flight, led to a further redesign. The blended wing canard layout of the XFV-12B was retained, but with rectangular augmenters incorporated into a design referred to as the XFV-12C. The wingspan was increased to retain acceptable longitudinal stability. Alterations were made to the arrangement of the main undercarriage housings, which were moved inboard of the wing box to retain the wing-fuselage attach structure, which had the effect that wing anhedral was reduced to a value of 8.8°. Ducting was basically similar to that suggested for the XFV-12B, with the exception of the canards, the ducting of which necessitated repositioning the canard augmenter outboard of that of the XFV-12A layout. Although the canard design was heavily modified over that of the XFV-12A design, the basic fuselage was not extensively changed in the XFV-12C – certainly not to the extent that had been incorporated into the XFV-12B. Estimated empty operational weight was 16,963 lb. (~7694 kg) (Rockwell International XFV-12A D&DP, 1981).

The various design studies that led to the XFV-12B (considered the most representative of an operational aircraft design) and XFV-12C indicated that it was possible to incorporate a thrust augmentation design, capable of high performance, into a V/STOL fighter aircraft design possessing conventional performance capabilities that were comparable to legacy aircraft (Rockwell International XFV-12A D&DP, 1981).

Although the drawing board designs showed potential for incorporating the rectangular augmenter designs into the confines of a tactical size V/STOL combat aircraft, neither the XFV-12B nor XFV-12C concepts were taken to the development stage. The writing had been on the wall for the XFV-12 program for some time prior to the emergence of the drawing board XFV-12B/C designs, as the thrust augmented wing concept was losing favour over the direct lift concept that had been proven on the P.1127 and later Kestrel and Harrier designs. The latter incorporated the AV-8A/C – shipboard testing of the AV-8A had commenced with the USN (United States Navy) in 1971 (Murphy *et al* c1970's & Aiken, 1977) and was in the process of being brought to fruition in the subsonic McDonnell Douglas (later Boeing) AV-8B (Harrier II) development program that would enter serial production for service with the USMC (United States Marine Corp) and foreign operators. The conclusion at NASA was that, although basic paper assessments indicated a capability increase over the subsonic Harrier (first generation) the XFV-12A design failed to produce enough thrust to be considered a viable V/STOL aircraft for an operational role (NASA). The AV-8B, second generation Harrier, would, alongside the CTOL (Conventional Take-Off and Landing) McDonnell Douglas (later Boeing) F/A-18A/B/C/D supersonic strike fighter, form the backbone of the USMC tactical aviation from the 1980's into the twenty first century, the F/A-18 also entering service with the USN.

The XFV-12A redevelopment phase of the program was brought to a sudden end in June 1981, before all of the program objectives had been tested/completed (Rockwell International XFV-12A D&DP, 1981). The deficiencies uncovered during the tethered hover testing at the IDRF – underperformance of the augmentation system and inadequate handling characteristics among the most serious – was a major influencing factor in the USN decision to cancel the XFV-12A program (Jackson *et al*).

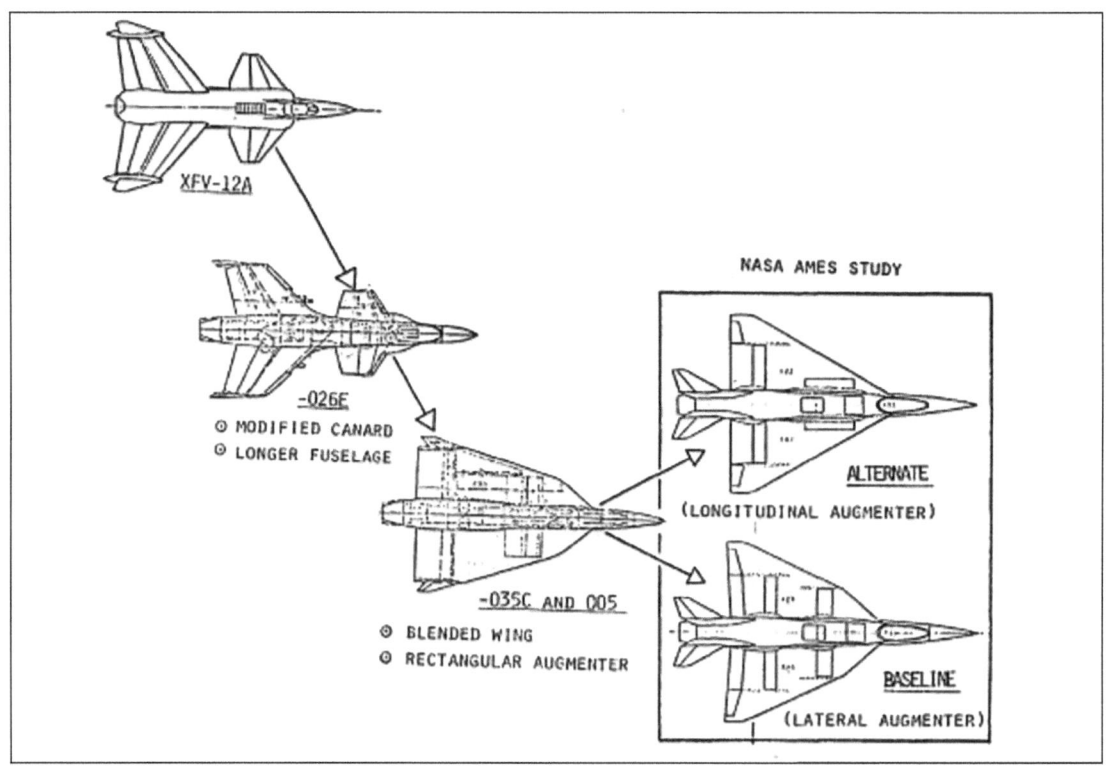

Design evolution from the XFV-12A to the single-cruise engine thrust augmented V/STOL designs studied on behalf of NASA Ames Research Center. Rockwell International (Boeing)/NASA Ames Research Centre

Post redevelopment and XFV-12 program cancellation, Rockwell International received contract NAS2-11002 from NASA Ames Research Center. This called for design studies (conducted in the period June 1981 to February 1982) into aerodynamic technology for a single-cruise engine V/STOL fighter/attack aircraft. The research built on work conducted on the XFV-12A program, but was primarily aimed at arriving at a design with a more advanced augmentation system (of rectangular design) than that tested in the XFV-12A prototype. The design study had been conducted in the wake of the XFV-12A redevelopment program (terminated in June 1981) and benefited from work conducted on the XFV-12B/C designs, which had not been brought to fruition. Ultimately, the designs that emerged during the study beyond the 026E (featuring a similar configuration to the XFV-12A, but with a modified canard and fuselage of increased length) emerged as the 035C and 005. These designs, which featured blended wing and rectangular augmenters (this was studied in two major variants featuring lateral augmenters (baseline model) and longitudinal augmenters (alternate model) respectively) were not brought to fruition, the program being terminated in February 1982 (Leon, 1982).

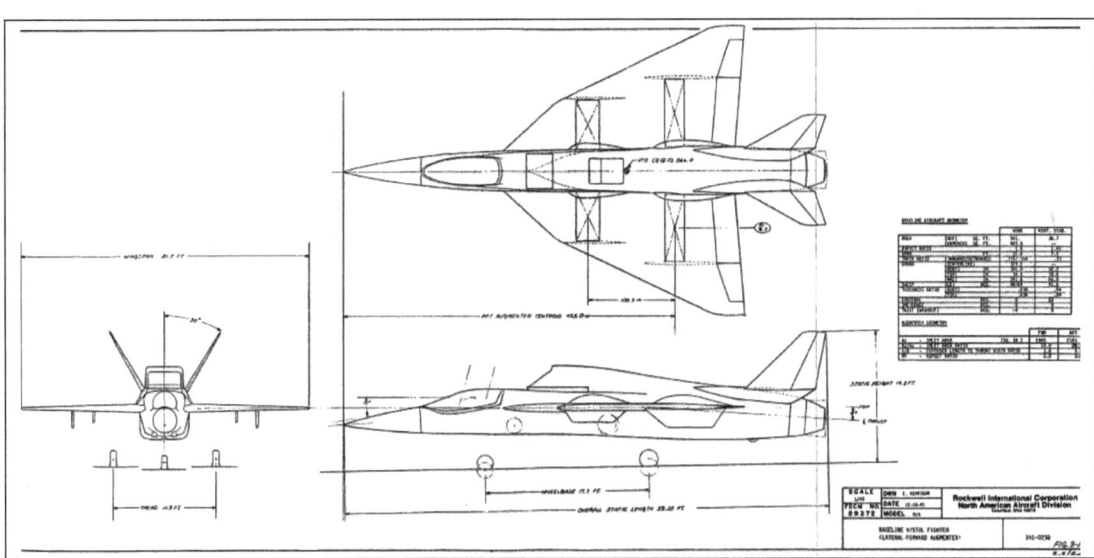

The Rockwell/Ames study spawned the 035C & 005. Depiction of the baseline model featuring lateral augmenters (top) and 3-view general arrangement (bottom). Rockwell International (Boeing)/Ames Research Centre

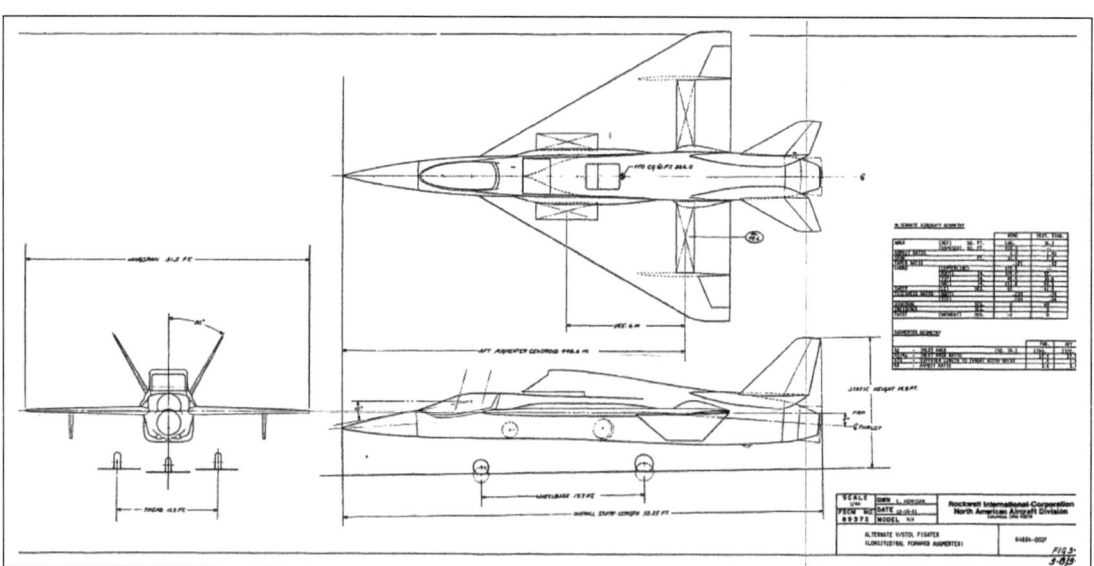

The Rockwell/Ames study spawned the 035C & 005. Rendering of the alternate model featuring longitudinal augmenters (top) and 3-view general arrangement (bottom). Rockwell International (Boeing)/Ames Research Centre

When the Rockwell study on behalf of Ames Research Centre ended in February 1982, it effectively ended Rockwell TAW programs potential of the thrust augmented wing concept to be taken forward to an operational application. As noted above, it would be direct lift that would win through with the AV-8B (lacking the supersonic capability mooted for, but not incorporated in, the XFV-12A) joining first generation Harrier and Soviet Yakovlev Yak-38M subsonic strike fighters as operational V/STOL designs operating from ship platforms.

McDonnell Douglas (Boeing)/British Aerospace (BAE Systems) AV-8B development aircraft. BAE Systems

The failure of the XFV-12A development program led to a downturn in interest/confidence, in the goal of creating a viable supersonic V/STOL strike fighter. However, this interest would be rekindled as the United States responded to the relative success of the Soviet Yakovlev Yak-41/141 supersonic strike fighter (relative in that the aircraft was successfully flight tested in a multitude of flight regimes, but suffered from excessive surface erosion when operating in ground effect). Ultimately, the Yak-41 did not advance to serial production, due to unresolved development issues and the back-scaling of Russian defence programs following the dissolution of the Soviet Union in December 1991. In the twenty first century the AV-8B (and derivatives) fleets would be replaced by the Lockheed Martin F-35B Lightning II (evolution of the X-35B demonstrator) V/STOL (still requiring a separate lift engine, which is redundant dead weight in cruise flight, with all the performance detriments that this entails), which had emerged through a plethora of studies from the ASTOVL (Advanced Short Take-Off and Vertical Landing) research program in the 1980's, the CALF (Common Affordable Lightweight Fighter) and JAST (Joint Advanced Strike Technology) programs of the 1990's through the X-32 and X-35 JSF (Joint Strike Fighter) demonstrators at the dawn of the twenty first century – the X-35B lift/plus lift cruise concept winning out over the Boeing X-32 direct lift design (Harkins, 2004, Harkins 2013 and Harkins 2013a).

Despite the promise that the thrust augmented wing design technology offered, the concept is effectively dormant in the twenty first century as far as incorporation into a high performance supersonic aircraft design is concerned. It remains to be seen whether the concept will be revived as technology advances and matures – stranger things have happened in the world of V/STOL aircraft design.

GLOSSARY

AFRL	Air Force Research Laboratory
AGM	Air to Ground [surface] Missile
AIM	Airborne Interception Missile
Anhedral	Descending inclination on the wing surface of an aircraft
ASTOVL	Advanced Short Take-off and Vertical Landing
ASW	Anti-Submarine Warfare
BBN	Balanced Beam Nozzle
CALF	Common Affordable Lightweight Fighter
Coanda	The coanda effect refers to a phenomenon whereby jet produced fluid excretes from outlet(s) and travels along an adjacent surface capturing foreign fluids/moisture to produce a locality of low-pressure
CTOL	Conventional Take-Off and Landing
D&DP	Diagnostic & Development Program
DTNRSDC	David Taylor Naval Ship Research and Development Center
Elevon	Moving part of a trailing-edge on certain types of aircraft wing
F	Fighter
FGR	Fighter Ground attack Reconnaissance
FRS	Fighter Reconnaissance Strike
ft.	Feet (foot) – unit of measurement
ft.^{2}	Feet (foot) squared – unit of measurement
ft./s	Feet per second
GE	General Electric
GR	Ground attack Reconnaissance
IDRF	Impact Dynamic Research Facility
III	Roman numeral number three
JAST	Joint Advanced Strike Technology
JSF	Joint Strike Fighter
kg	Kilogram
kg/f	Kilogram force
kg m^2	Kilogram per metre squared
kN	KiloNewton

lb.	Pound (unit of weight)
lb./f	Pound force
L/C	Lift/Cruise
L+L/C	Lift + Lift/Cruise
m	Metre
m^2	Metre squared
mm	millimetre
m/s	Metres per second
NASA	National Aeronautics and Space Administration
NASC	Naval Air Systems Command
PW	Pratt & Whitney
slug	Gravitational unit of mass within the foot per pound (lb). system. 1 lb. of force produces an acceleration of 1 ft. per second per second
STOL	Short Take-Off and Landing
TAW	Thrust Augmenting Wing
US	United States
USMC	United States Marine Corp
USN	United States Navy
V/STOL	Vertical Short Take-Off and Landing
VTOL	Vertical Take-Off and Landing
x	Times, multiplication
X	Experimental
XFV	Experimental Fighter Vertical
XV	Experimental Vertical
Yak	Yakovlev
$\pm$	Plus or minus
°	Degree(s)
~	Approximately equal to (can also be used to mean asymptotically equal)

BIBLIOGRAPHY

Aiken, Thomas N. (1977) 'Thrust Augmentor Application for STOL and V/STOL', NASA Technical Memorandum, Ames Research Centre, NASA Moffett Field, California

Baumann, K.J. & Swedlov, J.L. (1981) 'Research Priorities For Advanced Fibrous Composites', NASA Contractor Report 165414, Department of Mechanical Engineering, Carnegie-Mellon University, Pittsburgh, Pennsylvania

Bevilaqua, P.M. & Lee, J.D. (1980) 'Development of a Nozzle to Improve the Turning of Supersonic Coanda Jets: Technical Report AFWAL-TR-80-3027, Final Report for Period 15 June 1979-15 March 1980', Flight Dynamics Laboratory, Air Force Wright Aeronautical Laboratories, Air Force Systems Command, Wright-Patterson Air Force Base, Ohio

Culpepper, Richard. G, Murphy, Ronald. D, Gillespie, Edward. A & Lane, Archie G (1979) 'A Unique Facility for V/STOL Aircraft Hover Testing', NASA Technical Paper 1473, NASA Langley Research Centre, Hampton Virginia, Naval Air Systems Command, Washington D.C. and Rockwell International Corporation, Columbus Ohio

Delany, J.T. & Jenkins, G.M. (1976) 'XFV-12A Propulsion System Development', Rockwell International Corporation, Columbus Aircraft Division, Columbus, Ohio

Gerhardt, H.A. & Chen, W.S. (1978) 'Study of Aerodynamic Technology for V/STOL Fighter-Attack Aircraft – Vertical Attitude Concept', Northrop Corporation, Aircraft Group, Hawthorne, California, for NASA Ames Research Center, Moffett Field, California

Harkins, H. (2004) 'Lockheed Martin F-35 Joint Strike Fighter, The Universal Fighter', Centurion Publishing, United Kingdom

Harkins, H. (2013) 'X-35 – Progenitor to the F-35 Lightning II', Centurion Publishing, United Kingdom

Harkins, H. (2013) 'X-32 – The Boeing Joint Strike Fighter', Centurion Publishing, United Kingdom

Jackson, Karen E., Boitnott, Richard L. & Fasanella, Edwin L. (undated) 'A Summary of DoD-Sponsored Research Performed at NASA Langley's Impact Dynamic Research Centre, U.S. Army Research Laboratory, Vehicle Technology Directorate, Hampton, V.A.

Leon, M. (1982) 'Study of Aerodynamic Technology for Single-Cruise-Engine V/STOL Fighter/Attack Aircraft, NASA Contractor Report 166270, Rockwell International Corporation

Lopez, A.E., Koenig, D.G., Green, D.S. & Nagaraja, K.S. (1979) 'Workshop on Thrust Augmenting Ejectors', NASA Ames Research Centre, Naval Air Development Centre & Air Force Flight Dynamics Laboratory, held at Ames Research Centre, Moffett Field, California

Lowry, Randall B. (c1979) 'Interface concerns of ejector integration in V/STOL aircraft', Aeromechanics Division, Air Force Flight Dynamics Laboratory, Wright Patterson Air Force Base, Dayton, Ohio in Lopez, A.E., Koenig, D.G., Green, D.S. & Nagaraja, K.S. (1979) 'Workshop on Thrust Augmenting Ejectors', NASA Ames Research Centre, Naval Air Development Centre & Air Force Flight Dynamics Laboratory, held at Ames Research Centre, Moffett Field, California

Luidens, R, Plencer, R, Haller, W & Glassman, A. (1984) 'Supersonic STOVL Ejector Aircraft from a Propulsion Point of View', NASA Technical Memorandum 83641, Lewis Research Centre, Cleveland, Ohio

McCormick, Barnes. W. (c1970's) 'On the Status of V/STOL Flight', Department of Aerospace Engineering, Pennsylvania State University

Murphy, R & Lewis, Ernest L. (c1970's). 'XFV-12A Thrust-Augmented Wing (TAW) Prototype Aircraft', Naval Air System Command

NASA (undated) 'XFV-12A Wing Augmenter System and Component Diagnostic Testing Summary Report', NR75H-2, National Aeronautics and Space Administration

NASA CP-2001 (1976) 'Advances in Engineering Science, Volume 4, 12th Annual Meeting, Society of Engineering Science

NASA Langley Research Center (undated) 'XFV-12A NASA Langley Static and Dynamic Hover Tests Summary Report', NR78H-111, Langley Research Center

NASC & ARC (1977) 'Navy/NASA VSTOL Flying Qualities', Naval Air Systems Command, Naval Air Development Center, NASA Ames Research Center

Rockwell International (c1970's) 'XFV-12A V/STOL Technology Prototype', Rockwell International, Columbus Aircraft Division

Rockwell International (1973) 'High Speed Wind Tunnel Test of a 0.03 Scale Model of the XFV-12A Aircraft, Data Report', 73CL 2655, 6 March 1973, Rockwell International

Rockwell International (1973) 'High Speed Wind Tunnel Test of a 0.03 Scale Model of the XFV-12A Aircraft', 73CL 2976, 11 July 1973, Rockwell International

Rockwell International (1975) 'Low Speed Wind Tunnel Test of 0.20 Scale Powered Model of the XFV-12A, Data Report', 75CL 2104, 29 February 1975, Rockwell International

Rockwell International (1981) 'Summary report XFV-12A diagnostic and development program: Contract No. N00019-73-C-0053', North American Aircraft Division, Columbus, Ohio

Schum, E.J. & DeHart, J.H. (undated) 'Ejector Nozzle Development', Rockwell International, North American Aircraft Division

Stewart, V.R. (1981) 'A Study of a VTOL Thrusting Ejector in Low Speed Flight', NASA Contractor Report 166137, Rockwell International Corporation, Columbus, Ohio

Stewart, V.R. (1987) 'Low Speed Wind Tunnel Test of a Propulsive Wing/Canard Concept in the STOL Configuration, Volume 1: Test Description and Discussion of Results', NASA Contractor Report 178348, Rockwell International Corporation, Columbus, Ohio

Swavely, C.E. (1974) 'Engine Flow Diverter for the XFV-12A Prototype Aircraft', AIAA Paper No. 74-1194, AIAA/SAE 10th Propulsion Conference, 21-23 October 1974

Throndson, L.W. (1973) 'Compound Ejector Thrust Augmenter Development', ASME Paper No.73-FT-67

Watts, D.J, Sumida, P.T, Bunin, B.L., Janicki, G.S., Walker, J.V. & Fox, B.R. (1985) 'A Study of the Utilization of Advanced Composites in Fuselage Structures of Commercial Aircraft', Douglas Aircraft Company, Long Beach, California

ABOUT THE AUTHOR

Hugh Harkins FRAS is a geophysicist/historian and author with an extensive research/study background in aeronautic, astronautic, astrophysics, nautical and the wider scientific, technical and historical fields. He is also involved in research in the field of Scottish history, which formed significant elements of dual undergraduate degrees. Hugh has published in excess of sixty books, non-fiction and fiction, writing under his given name as well as utilising several pseudonyms. He has also written for several international magazines, whilst his work has been used as reference for many other projects, ranging from the aviation industry, international news corporations and film media to encyclopaedias, museum exhibits and the computer gaming industry. Hugh is a member of the Institute of Physics and is an elected Fellow of the Royal Astronomical Society. He currently resides in his native Scotland.

Other titles by the author include:

X-35 – Progenitor to the F-35 Lightning II
X-32 - The Boeing Joint Strike Fighter
Boeing X-36 Tailless Agility Flight Research Aircraft
XF-103 – Mach 3 Stratospheric Interceptor Concept
North American F-108 Rapier - Mach 3 Interceptor
Convair YB-60 - Fort Worth Overcast
Russia's Coastal Missile Shield - Bal-E & Bastion Mobile Coastal Cruise Missile Complexes
Iskander - Mobile Tactical Aero-Ballistic/Cruise Missile Complex
Orbital/Fractional Orbit Bombardment System - The Soviet Globalnaya Raketa
Counter-Space Defence Co-Orbital Satellite Fighter
Russia's Strategic Missile Carrier/Bomber Roadmap 2018-2040 – PAK DA, Tu-160M2, Tu-95MSM & Tu-22M3M
Sukhoi T-50/PAK FA - Russia's 5th Generation 'Stealth' Fighter
Sukhoi Su-35S 'Flanker' E - Russia's 4++ Generation Super-Manoeuvrability Fighter
Sukhoi Su-30MKK/MK2/M2 - Russo Kitashiy Striker from Amur
MiG-35/D 'Fulcrum' F – Towards the Fifth Generation
Air War over Syria, Tu-160, Tu-95MS & Tu-22M3 - Cruise Missile and Bombing Strikes on Syria, November 2015-February 2016
Sukhoi Su-27SM(3)/SKM
Russian/Soviet Aircraft Carrier & Carrier Aviation Design & Evolution Volume 1 - Seaplane Carriers, Project 71/72, Graf Zeppelin, Project 1123 ASW Cruiser & Project 1143-1143.4 Heavy Aircraft Carrying Cruiser
Soviet Mixed Power Experimental Fighter Aircraft – Piston-Liquid Propellant Rocket Engine/Piston-Ramjet/Piston-Pulsejet & Piston-Compressor Jet Engine Designs of the 1940's
Raid on the Forth - The First German Air Raid on Great Britain in World War II
Light Battle Cruisers and the Second Battle of Heligoland Bight
Into The Cauldron - The Lancaster MK.I Daylight Raid on Augsburg
Hurricane IIB Combat Log - 151 Wing RAF, North Russia 1941
RAF Meteor Jet Fighters in World War II, an Operational Log
Typhoon IA/B Combat Log - Operation Jubilee, August 1942
Defiant MK.I Combat Log - Fighter Command, May-September 1940
Blenheim MK.IF Combat Log - Fighter Command Day Fighter Sweeps/Night Interceptions, September 1939 - June 1940
Fortress MK.I Combat Log - Bomber Command High Altitude Bombing Operations, July-September1941
Light Battle Cruisers and the Second Battle of Heligoland Bight
British Battlecruisers of World War 1 - Operational Log, July 1914-June 1915

www.ingramcontent.com/pod-product-compliance
Lightning Source LLC
Chambersburg PA
CBHW042021150426
43197CB00003B/89